Chekhov's *Three Sisters*

Gordon McVay

Bristol Classical Press
Critical Studies in Russian Literature

First published in 1995 by
Bristol Classical Press
an imprint of
Gerald Duckworth & Co. Ltd
61 Frith Street
London W1D 3JL
e-mail: inquiries@duckworth-publishers.co.uk
Website: www.ducknet.co.uk

This impression 2002

A catalogue record for this book is available
from the British Library

ISBN 1-85399-382-4

Contents

For Mary and Bob

Introduction

Chekhov's richest and greatest play has inspired a bewildering variety of interpretations since its première at the Moscow Arts Theatre on 31 January 1901. *Three Sisters* (*Tri sestry*) has been viewed both as tragedy and as comedy, as a poignant testimony to the eternal yearning for love, happiness, beauty, and meaning, or as a devastating indictment of the folly of inert gentility and vacuous day-dreaming. Its characters have been deemed worthy embodiments of the universal 'human condition', keenly experiencing hope, disappointment, frustration, loneliness, and the passage of time – or passive products of pre-revolutionary Russian privilege, remnants fit only for the scrap-heap of history.

That the play has proved puzzling is hardly surprising, since Chekhov constantly shunned overt subjectivity and didacticism in his writings, just as he avoided ostentatious self-revelation in his personal life. Both as author and as man he appreciated the virtue of modesty and restraint. Like other plays of Chekhov's maturity, *Three Sisters* is multi-faceted and open-ended, rich in psychological and atmospheric nuance. To discern the dramatist's intentions requires – from reader and audience, director and cast – a corresponding delicacy of perception.

Detailed analysis of the text itself is of paramount importance (see Part One). Yet, since the play was not created by an automaton in a vacuum, it will be instructive first to consider briefly the author and his literary practice.

I

The outer facts of Chekhov's life are well established, thanks to his voluminous correspondence, the memoirs of relatives and acquaintances, and the efforts of scholars. Evidence suggests that, besides being a brilliantly innovative and subtle writer, he was also an unusually admirable person. Whereas other 'great' Russian authors incline to excess, with elements of neurosis and *folie des grandeurs* (Lermontov, Gogol, Dostoevsky, Tolstoy), Chekhov presents a remarkably unified and balanced personality, devoid of rhetoric and megalomania. In a land of preachers and partisans, he persistently refused to pontificate, with the result that he was often reviled for 'lack of principles' and absence of philosophical or political purpose. These charges worried him, although his life might serve as a model of positive practical endeavour. Despite his own ill-health,[1] he supported his family, treated peasants for their everyday ailments and at times of famine and cholera, planted trees, built schools, donated books to the Taganrog library, and performed innumerable undemonstrative acts of kindness.

There is an understandable temptation to regard Chekhov as a saintly figure, the gentle seer with tired, compassionate smile, pince-nez and blood-flecked beard. Yet, while not denying its attractiveness, virtually all biographers are struck by the 'elusiveness' of Chekhov's personality. His reticence may be interpreted as aloofness or detachment; his oft-repeated call for 'objectivity' as a writer may signify indifference; his playfully bantering tone in letters to enamoured females may betoken evasiveness and insensitivity; his gregariousness masks his loneliness; his concern may conceal an inner cold.

Some of these suspicions or accusations are not wholly without foundation. Chekhov devoted his limited energy to family, friends, creative work and charitable enterprise. It may well be that his equanimity and the early onset of his illness deprived him prematurely of youth's enviable elation. At the same time, however, his acute sense of proportion and his awareness of life's transience enabled him to see the folly of self-aggrandisement, and the vanity of rank, power and worldly success. 'Real talents always sit in the shadows', he wrote in March 1886.

His natural reserve was intensified by the application of will-power and self-control, as he endeavoured to protect his privacy and inner freedom. It has become almost commonplace to dub Chekhov an 'enigma', and a consequent legend has arisen of his total inscrutability. The fact remains, however, that the gregarious writer and doctor was usually surrounded by family and friends, and maintained a copious correspondence in addition to his output of stories and plays.

For a person supposedly 'isolated from others by a kind of inability to communicate, an impenetrability',[2] Chekhov proves an amazingly prolific correspondent. Between 1875 and 1904 he wrote more than 4,500 letters.[3] While it has been remarked that these missives are seldom, if ever,

---

1 Chekhov first coughed blood in 1884, and tuberculosis was finally diagnosed in 1897 after he suffered a massive lung haemorrhage.

2 Daniel Gillès, *Chekhov: Observer Without Illusion* (New York, 1968), p. 189.

3 For the fullest edition, see A.P. Chekhov, *Polnoe sobranie sochinenii i pisem v tridtsati tomakh* (Moscow, 1974-83), where the twelve volumes of letters contain some 4,500 items. Many other letters have perished, been deliberately destroyed, or remain undiscovered.

'confessional' (what else was he meant to 'confess'?), perhaps few people would disagree with the general assertion: 'Certainly the best source of information about the mind and soul of Chekhov, the man and the writer, is his own correspondence.'[4] Conversance with these letters may assist the reader to understand (or, at least, not grossly misunderstand) the essence of *Three Sisters*.

It was in 1888, towards the start of a two-year period of intense self-scrutiny, that Chekhov made his most famous pronouncement on truth and freedom:

> I'm afraid of people who try to read between the lines to find my 'tendency' and who will insist on viewing me as a liberal or conservative. I'm not a liberal, or a conservative, or a gradualist, or a monk, or an indifferentist. I should like to be a free artist and that's all, and I regret that God has not given me the strength to be one. I hate lies and violence of all kinds... My holy of holies is the human body, health, intelligence, talent, inspiration, love and the most absolute freedom imaginable, freedom from violence and lies, no matter what form these may take. That is the programme I would adhere to if I were a great artist...
>
> (*To A.N. Pleshcheev*, 4 October 1888)[5]

As the son of a despotic, provincial grocer and grandson of a serf, Chekhov was acutely conscious of the gulf between slavery and freedom. On one occasion, with apparent reference to his own painful evolution, he suggested as the theme for a short story the depiction of how a young man 'squeezes the slave out of himself drop by drop and then wakes up one fine morning to discover that in his veins flows not the blood of a slave, but of a real human being' (letter of 7 January 1889).[6] As a writer, Chekhov consistently rejected any manifestation of coercion. He was appalled by coarse and spiteful literary critics,

---

4 Carolina De Maegd-Soëp, *Chekhov and Women: Women in the Life and Work of Chekhov* (Ohio, 1987), p. 26.

5 Most of the quotations from Chekhov's letters may be found in *Chekhov: A Life in Letters*, translated and edited by Gordon McVay (The Folio Society: London, 1994).

6 It was perhaps his veneration of freedom which prompted him, in 1890, to undertake the unexpected and arduous journey across Siberia to Sakhalin, where he conducted a detailed census of some 10,000 convicts and settlers condemned to live out their lives in servitude.

and by the perniciousness of State censorship. Sectarianism repelled him.

Chekhov's private letters indicate that his profound respect for personal freedom was matched by his love of truth. In his published writings, however, he carefully avoided grandiloquent declarations, preferring to pose questions rather than impose answers. As a result, towards the end of the 1880s a number of critics (mainly journalists of a utilitarian, socially committed hue) began to assail him for his apparent failure to propound aims, ideals, opinions and 'solutions' in his works.

In response to such attacks, between 1888 and 1890 Chekhov gradually formulated his own concept of the dispassionate, objective, non-judgemental author. As a point of principle, he not only disclaimed authorial omniscience and the right or duty to moralise, but actually professed the positive value of disclosing one's own ignorance:

> It seems to me that one shouldn't expect writers to solve such questions as God, pessimism, and so on. The writer's task is simply to record how and in what circumstances somebody spoke or thought about God or pessimism. The artist should not be the judge of his characters and of what they say, but only an impartial witness. I heard a confused, totally inconclusive conversation of two Russians about pessimism and my duty is to convey this conversation exactly as I heard it, whereas the people to evaluate the conversation are the jury, that is, the readers. My only task is to be talented, that is, to know how to distinguish important evidence from the unimportant, to know how to illuminate characters and speak in their language... It's high time for writers, especially artists, to admit that in this world one can't understand anything, as Socrates once admitted, and Voltaire...
>
> (*To A.S. Suvorin*, 30 May 1888)

> You rebuke me for my objectivity, which you call indifference to good and evil, a lack of ideals and ideas, etc. When I depict horse-thieves, you want me to say: horse-stealing is wrong. But everyone knows that without me saying so! Let a jury judge them – my only task is to show them as they are... Whenever I write, I trust completely in my reader, and assume that he himself will add the subjective elements missing from my story...
>
> (*To A.S. Suvorin*, 1 April 1890)

Although Chekhov's scientific training and habitual scepticism inclined him towards non-didactic objectivity, he nevertheless remained deeply aware of the value of 'aims' for an author, and of the aimlessness characteristic of himself and the writers of his own generation (the 1880s and 1890s).[7]

From these, and similar, statements it might be tempting to deduce that the modestly undogmatic Chekhov was totally self-effacing in his writings. Indeed, he once advised his elder brother, Alexander (letter of 8 May 1889):

> Now – turning to your play... Above all, beware of the personal element. Your play will be no good whatsoever if all the characters resemble you... Who wants to know about my life and yours, my thoughts and your thoughts? Give people people – don't give them yourself...

If Chekhov's own personal sympathies were indeed entirely absent from his art, virtually all interpretations of his plays, including *Three Sisters*, might claim equal validity. Yet it should be realised that he cultivated 'indifference' and 'coldness' as a deliberate artistic method, to intensify the emotional effectiveness of his writing. He took pains to enlighten a fellow-author, Lidiya Avilova:

> Here's my advice as a reader: when you're portraying unfortunate wretches and want to rouse the reader's pity, try to be colder – that gives a kind of backdrop to the characters' grief, and will make it stand out more sharply. As things are, your heroes weep, and you sigh. Yes, be cold...
>
> (*Letter of 19 March 1892*)

> I wrote to you once that one has to be indifferent when writing sad stories. You didn't understand what I meant. One can weep and groan as one writes, and suffer along with one's heroes, but I think one must do so without the reader noticing. It makes a more powerful impression the more objective one is. That's what I meant...
>
> (*Letter of 29 April 1892*)

Despite his dispassionate air, Chekhov was never a totally neutral and impartial observer. As a writer, he had never pretended to be an unselecting lens, pointed at random to whatever passed before his eye. He assured Suvorin (letter of 27 October 1888):

---

7 See his letter to A.S. Suvorin (25 November 1892).

> An artist observes, selects, conjectures, arranges – and these very acts presuppose as their starting-point a question – for if from the start he's not set himself a question, there would be nothing to conjecture or select...
>
> In demanding that an artist should have a conscious attitude towards his work you are right, but you are confusing two concepts: *solving a question* and *posing a question correctly*. Only the latter is obligatory for an artist. There's not a single question solved in either *Anna Karenina* or *Onegin*, and yet they remain fully satisfying, simply because the questions they raise are all posed correctly. The court is obliged to pose the questions correctly, but let the jury decide, each according to his own taste...

Chekhov's seemingly 'uncommitted' tone, in works such as *Three Sisters*, may thus disguise or conceal a considerable amount of 'commitment', albeit of a non-partisan, non-strident kind. He was never a proponent of 'amoral' art:

> Literature is accepted as an art because it portrays life as it really is. Its aim is absolute and honest truth...[8]
>
> (*To M.V. Kiseleva*, 14 January 1887)

II

Anton Chekhov was a reluctant dramatist. For many years he saw himself primarily as a doctor, reiterating the formula: 'Medicine is my lawful wife, and literature is my mistress...' (11 September 1888).[9] Furthermore, in the realm of literature he felt more at ease with the short story than with the drama, once colourfully remarking: 'The narrative form is a lawful wife, whereas the dramatic form is a gaudy, loud-mouthed, brazen and tiresome mistress...' (15 January 1889).

Throughout his life Chekhov had an ambivalent attitude towards the stage. In one letter he described the contemporary Russian theatre as a 'vile

---

8 In a notebook, Chekhov observed: 'Man will become better when you show him what he is really like' (A.P. Chekhov, *Polnoe sobranie sochinenii i pisem v tridtsati tomakh: Sochineniia* XVII [Moscow, 1980], p. 90). Henceforth, references to the eighteen volumes of Chekhov's works will be cited from this edition thus: XVII, 90 (the Roman numeral denotes the volume, the Arabic indicates the page).

9 A similar thought is expressed in letters of, for instance, 17 January 1887, 11 February 1893, and 15 March 1896.

disease' which should be swept away (7 November 1888). When his first full-length play, *Ivanov*, received its memorably controversial première at Korsh's Theatre in Moscow on 19 November 1887, the dramatist was amazed by the actors' ad libbings and the director's 'blunders' (20 November 1887). Nine years later, at the first night of *The Seagull* (*Chaika*) he found the performers 'foul and foolish' (18 October 1896). He admired very few actors – Vera Komissarzhevskaya, Mariya Savina, to some extent Vladimir Davydov. Yet he loved the light-hearted vaudeville, and never fully lost his childhood enthusiasm, when he had frequented the Taganrog theatre and acted in amateur theatricals.

> You've become attached to the theatre, whereas I'm evidently drifting further and further away from it – and I regret that, for the theatre once afforded me much pleasure... Once upon a time I knew no greater delight than sitting in a theatre, but now I sit there with the sensation that someone up in the gods will call out at any moment: 'The building's on fire!' And I don't like actors. Being a playwright has spoilt me...
> (*To A.S. Suvorin*, 13 [25] March 1898)[10]

What particularly 'spoilt', and very nearly destroyed, his remaining benevolence towards the theatre was the disastrous Petersburg première of *The Seagull* on 17 October 1896. Chekhov never forgot his humiliation at the Alexandrinsky Theatre, after which he immediately vowed to abandon for ever the writing of plays. His letters indicate the extent of his hurt, and the vulnerability and wounded vanity of an essentially modest man.

> It's not the failure of my play which is to blame; after all, most of my earlier plays were failures too,[11] and that was

10 Chekhov was writing from Nice. The first date is according to the 'old style' Julian calendar used in Russia before the Revolution, and the second, according to the Gregorian calendar in use in Western Europe. In the nineteenth century, the Gregorian calendar was twelve days ahead of the Julian, and in the twentieth century, thirteen days ahead.

11 Critics attending the first night of *Ivanov* (19 November 1887) were predominantly hostile. The Petersburg revival of a substantially revised *Ivanov* (31 January 1889) was better received, but the Moscow première of *The Wood Demon* (*Leshii*) (27 December 1889) attracted much adverse comment, and the play was taken off after only five or six performances. At some unknown point between 1890 and 1896, Chekhov transformed *The Wood Demon* into a new play, *Uncle Vanya* (*Diadia Vania*). To date, his most popular (and lucrative) plays had been the one-act vaudevilles or 'jests', such as *The Bear*

> always like water off a duck's back. On 17 October it wasn't my play which failed – it was my whole person... I'm calm now, and in my usual frame of mind, but I still can't forget what happened, just as I couldn't, for instance, forget a blow in the face...
>
> (*To A.S. Suvorin*, 14 December 1896)

That Chekhov's 'pride was hurt' (letter of 22 October 1896) is hardly surprising, since he was offering the public his first new full-length play since *The Wood Demon* seven years earlier. First-night reviews of *The Seagull* were mainly hostile, and, despite its relative success on subsequent nights, the play was taken off after only five performances. For some time thereafter, it seemed that Anton Chekhov might never again write for the theatre.[12]

III

Although 1898 was an extremely productive year for Chekhov as a short-story writer, in the annals of theatrical history it is notable for marking the opening of his association with the newly established Moscow Arts Theatre. The initiative of its co-founders, K.S. Stanislavsky and Vl.I. Nemirovich-Danchenko, was to stimulate a remarkable late flowering of Chekhov the dramatist. On 17 December 1898, in its inaugural season, the Moscow Arts Theatre staged a highly successful revival of *The Seagull*, thereby easing somewhat the pain of the 1896 fiasco. On a more personal level, on 9 September 1898, Chekhov had admired for the first time a woman who was to play a central role in his final years: the actress Olga Leonardovna Knipper.

Chekhov missed the Moscow Arts Theatre première of *The Seagull*, as tuberculosis 'confined' him to Yalta, 'like Dreyfus on Devil's Island' (telegram to Nemirovich-Danchenko, 18 December 1898). When he eventually saw the production, at a special private performance in Moscow on 1 May 1899, he disliked the acting of Mariya Roksanova (Nina) and Stanislavsky (Trigorin), but was otherwise impressed.

Chekhov had already promised *Uncle Vanya* to the Maly Theatre, but when the Theatrical and Literary Committee (a kind of censorship body for

---

(*Medved'*) (1888) and *The Proposal* (*Predlozhenie*) (1888-9).

12 In the spring of 1897 Suvorin published an edition of Chekhov's plays (including *Uncle Vanya*), but Chekhov's letters between October 1896 and January 1899 indicate his reluctance to write any further plays.

the 'Imperial' theatres) demanded various changes if the work were to be staged at the 'Imperial' Maly Theatre, he promptly transferred his play to the privately owned Moscow Arts Theatre. Chekhov was able to admire a rehearsal of *Uncle Vanya* in Moscow on 24 May, but again the Arts Theatre première (on 26 October 1899) found him languishing in his Yalta 'exile'.

Confined to the south by illness, the writer yearned for Moscow, where there was culture, and the Moscow Arts Theatre, and the actress Olga Knipper. His letters document his growing attachment to the new theatre, which was helping to bring about his rebirth as a dramatist.

Having successfully revived *The Seagull* and mounted a major production of *Uncle Vanya*,[13] Stanislavsky and Nemirovich-Danchenko were naturally eager to commission an original work from Chekhov, the first play to be written specially for the Moscow Arts Theatre company. Earlier in 1899 the dramatist had already hinted at his willingness to comply.[14]

In a letter to Nemirovich-Danchenko on 24 November 1899 he mentioned for the first time the title, *Three Sisters*:

> I'm not writing any play. I have a theme, *Three Sisters* (*Tri sestry*), but until I finish the stories which have been on my conscience for a long time, I shan't start on the play...

Chekhov spent most of 1900 as a 'prisoner' in the Crimea, plagued by illness and unwanted visitors. There were, however, several highlights to punctuate the gloom. In April he joyfully greeted the Moscow Arts Theatre company when it toured Sevastopol and Yalta, performing, among other plays, his *Seagull* and *Uncle Vanya*. In July 1900 Olga Knipper stayed with the Chekhov family in Yalta, and the intimacy of their subsequent letters indicates that during this time the author and the actress became lovers. In the closing months of the year he struggled to complete his new play *Three Sisters*, which the Arts Theatre eagerly awaited for its 1900-1 season.

His letters from Yalta in 1900 chronicle the evolution of the play:

> Am I writing the new play? It's beginning to emerge, but I haven't started writing yet...
>
> (*To Vl.I. Nemirovich-Danchenko*, 10 March 1900)

> Yesterday Alekseev[15] visited me. We spoke of the play, I

---

13 *Uncle Vanya* had already been staged several times in the provinces in the second half of 1898.

14 See his letters of 8 February, 19 February and 8 October 1899.

15 The real name of K.S. Stanislavsky, who was born Konstantin Sergeevich

gave him my word, what's more I promised to finish the play no later than September...

(*To O.L. Knipper*, 9 August 1900)

My darling, I don't know when I'll be coming to Moscow – I don't know because, would you believe it, I'm now writing the play. Actually, it's not a play I'm writing, but more of a mess. There are lots of characters – perhaps I'll lose my way and abandon it...

(*To O.L. Knipper*, 14 August 1900)

I'm working in Yalta, not in Gurzuf, and people disturb me unmercifully, they disturb me vilely and abominably. The play's all in my head, it has already taken shape and levelled out, and is begging to be written down, but the moment I reach for my writing paper the door opens and some ugly mug crawls in...

(*To O.L. Knipper*, 18 August 1900)

I'm writing the play, but I'm afraid it will turn out boring...

(*To O.L. Knipper*, 23 August 1900)

Writing *Three Sisters* is very difficult, more difficult than my earlier plays... And writing's very difficult in Yalta; there are interruptions, and there seems no point in writing, and I don't like today what I wrote yesterday...

(*To his sister Masha*, 9 September 1900)

As for my play, it will be finished sooner or later, in September, or October, or even November, but I'm not sure whether to stage it this season... I'm not sure because, first, the play isn't quite ready – let it lie on my desk for a while, and, second, I must attend the rehearsals, I really must! I can't leave four important female roles, four educated young women, in Alekseev's hands, despite all my respect for his talent and insight. I must keep at least one eye on the rehearsals...

(*To O.L. Knipper*, 15 September 1900)

Alekseev, son of a wealthy textile manufacturer. Stanislavsky was his stage name.

> Oh, what a part I've got for you in *Three Sisters*! What a part![16] If you give me ten roubles you can have the part, otherwise I'll hand it over to another actress. I shan't offer *Three Sisters* this season. Let the play lie around for a bit and sweat, or – as merchants' wives say of a pie when they serve it up for dinner – let it breathe...
>
> (*To O.L. Knipper*, 28 September 1900)

> I'll probably make a fair copy of my new play when I'm in Moscow...
>
> (*To O.L. Knipper*, 4 October 1900)

> Would you believe it, I've written the play... It was terribly difficult to write *Three Sisters*. After all, it's got three heroines, each has to have her own shape and pattern, and all three are daughters of a general! The action takes place in a provincial town such as Perm, the milieu consists of soldiers, artillery...[17]
>
> (*To M. Gorky*, 16 October 1900)

On 23 October 1900 Chekhov arrived in Moscow, bringing with him the first version or draft of *Three Sisters*.[18] According to the memoirs of Olga Knipper, on 29 October Chekhov read his play to the Moscow Arts Theatre company, who reacted by claiming that it was only a 'sketch' or 'outline', with no fully developed 'roles'.[19] In Moscow he continued to revise the play:

---

16 The role of Masha in *Three Sisters* was written with Olga Knipper in mind.

17 Chekhov's first-hand knowledge of military circles is said to date back to his acquaintance with the family of Colonel B.I. Maevsky (the local battery commander) and Lieutenant E.P. Egorov in Voskresensk in 1883-4. See, for instance, M.P. Chekhov, *Vokrug Chekhova: Vstrechi i vpechatleniia* (Moscow, 1964), pp. 132-3. The army milieu is also reflected in Chekhov's story *The Kiss* (*Potselui*) (1887).

18 A comparison of this first, 'Yalta', version of *Three Sisters* and the 'final text' is most revealing. See the valuable publication by A.R. Vladimirskaya, 'Dve rannie redaktsii p'esy "Tri sestry"', in *Literaturnoe nasledstvo*, LXVIII: *Chekhov* (Moscow, 1960), pp. 1-86. For ease of reference, variants in Chekhov's text will be quoted from the notes to Volume XIII of his thirty-volume collected works (Moscow, 1978): XIII, 273-309.

19 O.L. Knipper-Chekhova, in *Chekhov v vospominaniiakh sovremennikov* (Moscow, 1954), p. 606. Other sources (including Stanislavsky and Nemirovich-Danchenko) indicate that, although Chekhov attended this reading on 29 October, he himself did not recite the play. Chekhov's lifelong distaste for public declamation is well attested.

> *Three Sisters* is finished... The play has turned out dull, protracted and awkward; I say – awkward, because, for instance, it has four heroines and a mood, as they say, gloomier than gloom itself...
>
> My play is complex like a novel and its mood, people say, is murderous...
>
> (*To V.F. Komissarzhevskaya*, 13 November 1900)

The ailing author left Moscow on 11 December 1900, arriving in Nice three days later. At the Pension Russe he continued his work on *Three Sisters*:

> The windows in my room are wide open; and it seems as if my soul too is wide open. I'm copying out my play and feel amazed at how I could write this piece, and what for...
>
> I'll go down to the sea now, I'll sit there and read the newspapers, and then, when I come home, I'll copy out the play – and tomorrow I'll be able to send Nemirovich Act III, and the day after tomorrow Act IV – or both of them together...[20]
>
> (*To O.L. Knipper*, 15 [28] December 1900)

> In Act III I've changed only a little, but in Act IV I've made drastic changes. I've added many words for you...
>
> (*To O.L. Knipper*, 17 [30] December 1900)

> The play is now finished and I've sent it off...
>
> (*To O.L. Knipper*, 21 December 1900 [3 January 1901])

While the Moscow Arts Theatre company was rehearsing *Three Sisters*,[21] Chekhov sent further letters from Nice. Although willing to comment on specific details of the action and characterisation, he was reluctant to elaborate on the play's overall mood or 'message':

> You write that in Act III, when Natasha is making her rounds of the house at night, she puts out the lights and looks for

---

20 Chekhov sent off Act III to Moscow on 16 December 1900, and Act IV on 20 December.

21 Stanislavsky's meticulous work as director is recorded in his production score of *Three Sisters* – see *Rezhisserskie ekzempliary K.S. Stanislavskogo*, III: *1901-1904: P'esy A.P. Chekhova 'Tri sestry', 'Vishnevyi sad'* (Moscow, 1983), pp. 87-289. Henceforth, references to Stanislavsky's production score will cite the page only of this edition.

> burglars under the furniture. But I think it would be better if she strode straight across the stage, *à la* Lady Macbeth, clutching a candle – that would be crisper and more horrifying...[22]
>
> (*To K.S. Stanislavsky*, 2 [15] January 1901)

> Indeed, Solyony thinks he looks like Lermontov; but of course he doesn't – the very idea is laughable... He should be made up to look like Lermontov. The resemblance to Lermontov is enormous, but it exists only in Solyony's mind...[23]
>
> (*To I.A. Tikhomirov*, 14 [27] January 1901)

> Of course, you're absolutely right. Tuzenbakh's corpse shouldn't be shown at all. I felt this myself when I was writing, and spoke to you about it, if you remember.[24] As for the end being like *Uncle Vanya* – that's no great misfortune. After all, *Uncle Vanya* is my play, and not somebody else's, and when one echoes oneself in a work, people say that's how things should be...
>
> (*To K.S. Stanislavsky*, 15 [28] January 1901)

With his typical love of understatement, Chekhov encouraged a subtle discernment in all aspects of the production:

---

22 In his reply later in January Stanislavsky explained: 'Natasha looks for burglars not in the third, but in the second act'. Natasha appears with a candle on two occasions in Act II (at the beginning and towards the end), and once in Act III (towards the end). The two men seem to be talking of different episodes – Stanislavsky evidently wanted Natasha to look for miscreants at the beginning of Act II, whereas Chekhov wished her to cross the stage '*à la* Lady Macbeth' late in Act III.

23 On one level, Solyony may be regarded as a psychopathic murderous misfit, a tragi-comic parody of the Lermontovian hero. Lermontov (1814-41) was Russia's greatest Romantic poet.

24 In the 'Yalta' version of the play, Chekhov's stage direction towards the end of Act IV included the words: 'there is a noise at the back of the stage; a crowd can be seen, looking on as the body of the Baron, who has been killed in the duel, is carried past' (XIII, 308). This stage direction led to a lively correspondence between Chekhov and Stanislavsky, both of whom seem determined to persuade the other to drop the idea (the Moscow Arts Theatre stage was too small, the spectacle of a corpse would distract from the mood of the sisters' closing speeches, etc.). See also Chekhov's letter to O.L. Knipper on 20 January (2 February) 1901. The episode was wisely excluded from the final version.

> Of course, Act III must be performed quietly, to convey the feeling that people are exhausted, and that they want to sleep... What noise are you talking about? I've indicated where bells should be ringing off-stage.[25]
>
> (*To O.L. Knipper*, 17 [30] January 1901)

> You write that in Act III there is noise and bustle... What do you mean? The noise and bustle are only in the distance, off-stage, a vague muffled noise, but here on stage everyone's exhausted, almost asleep... If you spoil Act III the play will be ruined and I'll be hissed off the stage in my old age...
>
> (*To O.L. Knipper*, 20 January [2 February] 1901)

> Masha's confession in Act III is not a real confession, but merely a candid conversation. Play it with agitation, but not despair, don't shout, do smile from time to time and, above all, play it in such a way that one can feel the exhaustion of night. And also so that one can feel you're cleverer than your sisters, or at least that you regard yourself as cleverer...
>
> (*To O.L. Knipper*, 21 January [3 February] 1901)

> You inform me that in Act III you lead Irina by the arm... What for?... Can't Irina cross the stage by herself?...
>
> (*To O.L. Knipper*, 24 January [6 February] 1901)

> I'm leaving for Italy at 12 midnight...
>
> (*To O.R. Vasilieva*, 26 January [8 February] 1901)

Chekhov duly arrived in Pisa:

> I'm writing this to you from Pisa, my darling. From here I'll be going to Florence, then Rome, and then Naples...
>
> Was my play performed or not? I know nothing...
>
> (*To O.L. Knipper*, 28 January [10 February] 1901)

On 31 January 1901, while Chekhov was in his beloved Italy, the première of *Three Sisters* took place in Moscow.

---

25 In her letter to Chekhov on 11 January 1901 Olga Knipper had written that, when rehearsing Act III, Stanislavsky had emphasised 'a terrible commotion on stage, with everyone running about feverishly...'.

Part One

Commentary to *Three Sisters*

The Plot

On the surface, there is nothing particularly obscure about the plot of *Three Sisters*. Set in a provincial town with 100,000 inhabitants, the play depicts the lives and aspirations of the Prozorov[1] family (three sisters and a brother) and their assorted friends (mainly military). Frustrated and dissatisfied with their present existence, the Prozorovs recall past happiness in Moscow, which they left eleven years before the drama begins, and long to return there to attain future happiness. Olga, the eldest sister (aged twenty-eight), a conscientious but harassed schoolteacher, yearns to be married; Masha, the middle sister, loathes her pedantic, kindly husband, the Latin teacher, Kulygin; Irina, the youngest (aged twenty), seeks fulfilment in work and love. As daughters of a recently deceased general, the sisters have high expectations of life, and their brother, Andrei, dreams of becoming a

1 Most of the characters in *Three Sisters* may be formally listed by their first name, patronymic (son or daughter of), and surname – thus, Andréi Sergéevich (son of Sergéi) Prózorov, Maríya Sergéevna (daughter of Sergéi) Prózorova (female surnames usually add an 'a'), and so on. Various first names also have familiar or affectionate diminutive forms – thus, Maríya Sergéevna is known in the family as Másha. Patronymics may be contracted (to Sergéich, Ignátyich, Vasílyich, Románych). One character (Anfísa) is identified by first name only, and the surname of two others (Natálya Ivánovna and Ferapónt Spiridónych) is not given.

The full cast list, with certain diminutives indicated in brackets, is as follows: Andréi Sergéevich Prózorov (Andryúsha, Andryúshka, on one occasion Andryushánchik); Natálya Ivánovna (Natásha); Ólga Sergéevna Prózorova (Ólya, Ólechka, Ólyushka); Maríya Sergéevna Prózorova (married surname Kulýgina) (Másha, Máshenka); Irína Sergéevna Prózorova; Fyódor Ilyích Kulýgin (Fédya); Alexánder Ignátyevich Vershínin; Nikolái Lvóvich Tuzenbákh (or Túzenbakh, if stressed on the first syllable as in the original German Tusenbach); Vasíly Vasílyevich Solyóny; Iván Románovich Chebutýkin; Alexéi Petróvich Fedótik; Vladímir Kárlovich Rodé; Ferapónt Spiridónych; Anfísa. Others to appear include Bóbik and Sófochka, and among the unseen characters is Mikhaíl Iványch Protopópov.

professor at Moscow University.

In the course of four acts, spanning several years, happiness proves elusive. Olga becomes a reluctant headmistress while remaining unmarried; Masha has an affair with Lieutenant-Colonel Vershinin, and is grief-stricken when he departs; Irina, disheartened by prosaic routine work, agrees to marry the ugly Baron Tuzenbakh – yet he is killed the day before their wedding. Andrei marries a local girl, Natasha, who is unfaithful and domineering, gradually expelling the Prozorovs from their family home. Despite these disappointments, however, the sisters do not despair. In a final tableau, while the drunken doctor, Chebutykin, expresses his customary nihilistic indifference, the three sisters stand together, determined to live, to work, and to discover the meaning of their suffering.

Any plot synopsis is inevitably selective, and this is especially true of a play such as *Three Sisters*, which teems with significant (or insignificant) detail. Confronted by a typically Chekhovian blend of triviality and profundity, 'relevance' and 'irrelevance', the reader or theatre-goer has to respond to fragmented dialogue, fluctuating moods, and complicated relationships. For those accustomed to the certainty of dramatic conflict and resolution *Three Sisters* may appear as something of a puzzle, with its inconclusive conclusion, its 'subtext' and 'undercurrents'.[2]

By the autumn of 1900, when he came to write his penultimate play, Chekhov had largely dispensed with many stock ingredients of traditional drama, such as a firm plot-line, the concentration on one central protagonist, a sharp division into 'positive' and 'negative' characters ('heroes' and 'villains'), artificial soliloquies, contrived set-pieces lucidly debating some crucial issue, and the inexorable progression towards a theatrical climax and a satisfying dénouement.

Nevertheless, his manner of writing was scarcely 'revolutionary'. *Three Sisters* is clearly recognisable as a four-act family drama, with an evolving plot (or abundance of evolving sub-plots) and a realistic setting. No individual part, however, dominates the whole. The intricacy of Chekhov's text raises thoughts of 'ensemble playing' and 'orchestration'.

Analogies with other art forms readily arise. Over half a century ago one critic was reminded of conductors, poets and painters (Manet, Vuillard,

---

2 *Podtekst* (subtext, concealed meaning) and *podvodnoe techenie* (undercurrent[s]) have – like *nastroenie* (mood, atmosphere) – become clichés of Chekhovian criticism. These terms were already used in the early years of this century, by Nemirovich-Danchenko, Stanislavsky, and numerous other writers.

Utrillo): 'It is part of this drama's genius to make you think in terms of other media – of lilts and cadences, of brushwork, of wind and strings.'[3] A contemporary agreed, while hailing *Three Sisters* as 'the best' of all Chekhov's plays:

> It has the unanalysable appeal of music as well as the absorbing interest of a story... Each character like an instrument in an orchestra leads or gives way in turn; sometimes playing alone, sometimes with others and scarcely heard...[4]

The subtle delicacy of Chekhov's writing precludes any single, 'correct' interpretation. Yet the dramatist himself was deeply distressed by wilful or ignorant misinterpretations. According to Stanislavsky (one of the co-directors of the first production), there was immediate disagreement about the very essence of *Three Sisters*:

> Finally Chekhov came himself with the fourth act, and a reading of the play was arranged, with the author present... After the reading of the play, some of us, in talking of our impressions of the play, called it a drama, and others even a tragedy, without noticing that these definitions amazed Chekhov...
>
> Confused, hurt, and even insulted, he left the meeting, trying to go out without being noticed... Afraid that it was his state of health that had forced him to leave the Theatre, I went at once to his home and found him not only out of spirits and insulted, but angry. I do not remember ever seeing him so angry again...
>
> The real reason was that he had written a happy comedy and all of us had considered the play a tragedy and even wept over it. Evidently Chekhov thought that the play had been misunderstood and that it was already a failure...[5]

Stanislavsky's memory seems somewhat faulty here. While Chekhov may well have objected to the portentous title of 'tragedy' (and the copious shedding of tears), he can hardly have really believed that he had created a

---

3 James Agate, *The Sunday Times* (30 January 1938).

4 Desmond MacCarthy, *The New Statesman and Nation* (5 February 1938), p. 206.

5 Constantin Stanislavsky, *My Life in Art*, translated by J.J. Robbins (London, 1924), pp. 370-1.

'happy comedy'.[6] Moreover, whereas he had himself designated *The Seagull* as a 'comedy' (*komediia*),[7] and described *Uncle Vanya* as 'scenes from country life', he specifically called *Three Sisters* by the more neutral term 'drama' (*drama*). In this drama, unmistakably serious themes are punctuated with laughter, for nothing could be further from Chekhov's art than unrelieved earnestness and unsmiling solemnity.

The 'meaning' of the play gradually unfolds through the steady accumulation of detail, from the opening curtain to the final tableau. For the reader and the spectator it is a passage from total ignorance to partial knowledge. One possible approach for a critic (which mirrors the experience of reader and spectator) is to trace the progression of each act, interpreting in turn the significance of almost every comment, conversation, and configuration of character, and noting where necessary the recurrence of certain ideas and patterns. This method has already been practised by various scholars, and, if rigorously applied, could lead to a monograph of several hundred pages, since the richness of Chekhov's text is virtually inexhaustible.

An alternative approach, however, may be equally, or even more, illuminating – that of standing back from the sequence of words and reflecting in tranquillity upon the wider scene. If the texture of *Three Sisters* is reminiscent of a symphony, conveying, perhaps, 'the still, sad music of humanity',[8] it may be particularly valuable to identify the themes and leitmotifs which permeate the play. Accordingly, after a brief further outline of the unfolding plot, the emphasis will rest upon broader issues.

Although an attempt will be made to avoid deliberate distortion, it remains as difficult for a critic (or reader or spectator) to be 'impartial' and 'objective' as it is for the creative writer. To paraphrase Chekhov's letter of 27 October 1888 (substituting 'critic' for 'artist'): 'A *critic* observes, selects, conjectures, arranges...'.

Finally, since no critic is sole possessor of the one truth, both author and reader of this study might heed the wisdom of Chekhov's remarks (letter of 19 March 1892): 'In any case, take no notice of me, I'm a bad critic. I don't

---

6 This seems clear from Chekhov's letter of 13 November 1900, where he does not dispute the opinions he quotes: 'The play has...a mood, as they say, gloomier than gloom itself... Its mood, people say, is murderous...'. However, in a letter to Z.S. Sokolova on 7 September 1901 Stanislavsky wrote of Chekhov: 'He still thinks even now that *Three Sisters* is a highly cheerful piece (*preveselen'kaia veshchitsa*)'.

7 Similarly, he was to call his last play, *The Cherry Orchard* (*Vishnevyi sad*) a 'comedy', maintaining in a letter of 15 September 1903 that 'it has turned out to be not a drama, but a comedy, in places even a farce...'.

8 From William Wordsworth's 'Lines composed a few miles above Tintern Abbey' (1798).

have the knack of formulating my critical thoughts lucidly. Sometimes I talk such nonsense, it's absolutely dreadful...'.

Act I

The play opens in springtime, in the drawing-room of the Prozorovs' house, in a provincial town far from Moscow. It is 5 May, Irina's twentieth birthday,[9] and various factors suggest a mood of buoyancy and expectation – the cheerful midday sun, Irina's white dress and youthful optimism, the table already set for a festive celebration, and, later, Vershinin's arrival, the family gathering around the laden table, and Andrei's exuberant proposal of marriage to Natasha. Several characters express a yearning for love, and marriage, and satisfying work, and Moscow. Yet any hopefulness is counterbalanced by other features – the remembrance of dead parents, Olga's perpetual headaches and frustrated spinsterhood, Masha's black dress and gloomy whistling, Chebutykin's indifference and Solyony's awkwardness, Kulygin's pedantry, the unseen menace of Protopopov, and the pervasive awareness of passing time. This balance of light and shade, hope and despair, is to continue throughout the play.

Act II

It is past 8 o'clock in the evening, with the darkness barely dispersed by one lit candle. The set remains unaltered, and Natasha and Andrei are still on stage. It soon becomes clear, however, that much has happened since the betrothal kiss which ended Act I. Andrei and Natasha, now man and wife, have a baby son, Bobik – but their marriage seems almost dead. It is carnival time, February, presumably some twenty-one months since Irina's sunlit twentieth birthday.[10] Time has begun to wreak disappointment. Irina feels unfulfilled by work at the post office,[11] and unimpressed by her two persistent suitors, Tuzenbakh and Solyony. Andrei has taken to gambling, Olga is exhausted by unsought obligations as deputy headmistress, and Chebutykin senses the burden of loneliness. Yet hope and expectation survive – Irina still dreams of Moscow; Masha and Vershinin, each trapped in unhappy wedlock, turn to one another for consolation; Vershinin and Tuzenbakh continue to philosophise about the future happiness of mankind;

---

9 More precisely, it is Irina's name-day (*imeniny*, the feast-day of the saint after whom a person is named). The feast-day of St Irene (a martyr of Thessalonica, burnt at the stake under the Roman emperor Diocletian, *c.* 300) is celebrated on 5 May.

10 For a play so rich in time references, the dramatist evidently takes delight in concealing the exact time-lapse between each act.

11 More literally, telegraph office (*telegraf*).

and, more immediately, the carnival mummers are eagerly awaited. The disruptive Natasha, however, is becoming increasingly dominant. After asking Irina to move into Olga's room (to make way for baby Bobik) and banishing the festive mood by cancelling the mummers' party, she dons a fur coat and exits, to enjoy a little drive with Protopopov.

Act III

The long day's journey into night leads to ever deepening disillusionment. It is past 2 o'clock in the morning, with sounds of off-stage bustle and the glow of a summer fire which has destroyed some neighbouring houses. On-stage, in the room now shared by Olga and Irina, everyone is exhausted. A further year and more has passed – Natasha has produced her second child, a daughter, Sofochka, and Irina is already twenty-three. While Natasha's fortunes rise (as she dominates the household and continues her liaison with Protopopov), the Prozorovs seem in disarray, with their dreams and ideals unachieved. Olga remains unloved; Masha snatches at happiness with Vershinin; Irina wilts and pines. Their cuckolded, non-professorial brother has mortgaged the house, and works for the county council, under Protopopov. As tensions mount and nerves become strained, various characters (Irina, Masha, Andrei) give voice to their concealed yearnings and near-despair. The immediate future is clouded by the possible imminent departure of the brigade, which will remove Vershinin from Masha and the company of amiable soldiers from the household. The curtain falls with Irina agreeing to marry Baron Tuzenbakh (even though she does not love him) and longing still for Moscow.

Act IV

Time has turned full circle, to midday once more, but instead of spring sunlight and Vershinin's arrival in Act I, it is now chill autumn and the season of departure. The action takes place out of doors, in the old garden belonging to the Prozorovs' house, near a terrace and an avenue of fir-trees. Natasha's usurpation of the house appears complete – while her lover, Protopopov, remains unseen inside, the three sisters have no wish to re-enter her domain. Olga, now headmistress, lives at the school, where she provides a refuge for the elderly Anfisa. Irina (although anxious about some mysterious quarrel between Solyony and the Baron) hopes to marry Tuzenbakh on the following day, and then embark with him upon a life of work. An elegiac mood pervades this final act, as characters bid farewell, perhaps never to meet again. Lovers and non-lovers part. The unloved Tuzenbakh takes his leave of the unloving Irina, and Vershinin bestows a lingering last kiss upon the distraught Masha. Others are merely onlookers – Chebutykin, Olga, Kulygin, whom no one loves. As Natasha plans to chop down the fir-trees, and a military band plays a march off-stage, Chebutykin enters to announce the death of Tuzenbakh, shot in a duel by his jealous rival, Solyony. While the doctor expresses his habitual indifference, and Andrei pushes a pram, and Kulygin smiles contentedly now that Vershinin has departed, the three sisters stand close together, resolved to live, and to work, and to find out why they live and suffer.

The Characters

It has become something of a cliché to regard the characters of Chekhovian drama as introverted and isolated, passive and inert, failures snared in wistful, autumnal worlds of their own. This over-simplification bears as much resemblance to the truth as does one scholar's description of Anton Chekhov himself as 'that melancholy bard of his crepuscular land', 'the tired wanderer, who ardently wished to live, but had never learned the secret of living': 'It was in a queer world of silvery twilight and dark shadows that the gentle soul of Chekhov took refuge, in a desperate fear of life... Weakness of body paralyzed his will and kept him in strange dim realms of twilight... Chekhov's life is the story of perpetual disillusionment...'[12]

Unlike those victims of late twentieth-century mechanisation, who may indeed appear to dwell in 'strange dim realms of twilight', caught in a faceless world of commuters and computers, the overriding impression conveyed by the characters of *Three Sisters* is that they are highly individualised, while also forming part of a kind of extended family, meeting frequently in social gatherings.[13] As individuals, they may suffer from loneliness and frustration, and the inevitable self-centredness of personal unhappiness, and yet in many respects they share a common destiny, and feel sympathy for one another's plight, as well as powerlessness to help.

An initial glance at the cast list reveals that – as Chekhov himself observed in his letter of 14 August 1900 – there are 'lots of characters'. No fewer than fourteen people are mentioned in the *dramatis personae* (nine male, five female), and yet it is relatively easy to picture these diverse characters, for they are introduced gradually by the dramatist and, with one minor exception, appear in each of the four acts.[14] Moreover, unlike the stereotypical figures of a didactic, socio-political drama,[15] the characters in

12 Princess Nina Andronikova Toumanova, *Anton Chekhov: The Voice of Twilight Russia* (New York, 1937), pp. 105, 137, 8, 95.
13 Hence a skilled ensemble of actors is required, to embody this closely knit group.
14 The exception is Rodé, who is absent from Act III.
15 Such as Maxim Gorky's *Enemies* (*Vragi*) (1906).

Three Sisters breathe the complexity and mystery of life itself. They demonstrate the truth of Ivanov's comment to Dr Lvov (in Act III of *Ivanov*): 'No, doctor, we all have too many wheels, screws and valves in us to judge each other on first impressions or two or three outer signs...'.

When approaching the characters of *Three Sisters*, one might also heed Chekhov's own declaration (in a letter to Suvorin on 3 November 1888):

> Dividing people into successes and failures means looking at human nature from a narrow and prejudiced angle... Are you a success or not? Am I? And Napoleon? And your Vasily?[16] What's the criterion? One would need to be God to separate the successes accurately from the failures...

Nevertheless, it seems most improbable that the dramatist viewed all the characters in *Three Sisters* with equal benevolence.

In his letter to Maxim Gorky on 16 October 1900 Chekhov had remarked: 'It was terribly difficult to write *Three Sisters*. After all, it's got three heroines, each has to have her own shape and pattern, and all three are daughters of a general!...' Olga, Masha and Irina are on stage at the opening and close of the play, their trinity thus providing a framework for the entire action. The main leitmotifs (such as love, marriage, work, happiness, time, Moscow and meaning) are indissolubly linked with the three sisters, but before these themes are examined in turn, a brief portrait might be offered of the characters' separate personalities.

When the curtain rises on Act I, to reveal the three sisters clad in contrasting colours (Olga's regulation blue as a teacher, Masha's doleful black as a grieving spouse,[17] and Irina's virginal, vernal white), it is Olga, the eldest sister, who speaks first. She too will eventually utter the play's concluding words, which seems particularly apt, since Olga is a reassuring presence, solicitous and kind, who selflessly presides over the entire Prozorov family. Careworn, conscientious, emotionally unspent and prematurely ageing, Olga lacks the forcefulness to relish the rigours of schoolteaching or to resist the intrusion of Natasha.[18] Laudably free from

---

16 Suvorin's manservant.

17 Chekhov may be consciously echoing the other black-clad Masha, who blatantly paraded her misery at the start of *The Seagull*.

18 Audiences are always shocked early in Act III, when Olga proves powerless to protect Anfisa from Natasha's onslaught. Olga is not, however, inactive or defeatist – she selects clothes for the fire victims in Act III, and rescues Anfisa in Act IV by providing her with a room and bed in the school flat.

careerist ambition, she is drafted into the position of deputy headmistress when the headmistress falls ill (Act II), and by Act IV has become permanent headmistress, perhaps partly due to the machinations of Natasha and Protopopov.[19] She is so patently a wife and mother *manquée*, who would indeed have loved even an aged husband (as she admits to Irina in Act III). Her tenderness remains untapped, while her sisters are pursued by suitors. Olga's life serves to illustrate her dictum (Act IV) that 'nothing ever happens as we'd like it to'.[20]

The middle sister, Masha, forms a marked contrast with the unostentatious and unglamorous Olga. Masha is the most passionate, hot-tempered and full-blooded of the sisters, confronting life's adversity with a flinty, sullen defiance. Whereas Olga seems condemned to perpetual spinsterhood, and Irina has not realised her romantic dreams, Masha openly spurns the boring, kindly husband she married when only eighteen, and responds with increasing fervour to the newly arrived Vershinin. In his letter to Olga Knipper on 2 (15) January 1901, Chekhov had advised the actress:

> Ah, take care! Don't put on a sad face in any of the acts. Angry, yes, but not sad. People who have known grief for a long time and grown used to it merely whistle softly from time to time,[21] and often become pensive. So you too should try to look pensive quite often on stage, during conversations. Do you understand?...[22]

---

19 Early in Act III, when Olga denies that she will become headmistress, Natasha confidently retorts: 'You'll be chosen, Olechka. It's already settled.' As chairman of the county council, Protopopov may have arranged the appointment. It certainly suits Natasha and him that Olga should live in the headmistress' flat at school, rather than remain within the Prozorov household.

20 Literally: 'Everything happens not in accordance with our plans/wishes/desires' (*Vsë delaetsia ne po-nashemu*). All quotations from *Three Sisters* are translated by Gordon McVay.

21 Although Chekhov himself claimed to be 'a cheerful person' (letter of 6 [18] October 1897), he used the same verb for habitual whistling (*posvistyvat'*) in a letter to Gorky on 18 January 1899: 'You write that I'm stern. I'm not stern. I'm lazy – I just wander about, whistling from time to time...'.

22 On 2 January 1900 Chekhov had written to Olga Knipper: 'Suffering should be expressed on stage as it is in life – that is, not via arms and legs, but in the tone of voice, or a glance; not with gesticulation, but with grace. The subtle emotions characteristic of cultured people should be expressed externally in a subtle way too...'.

Whereas the long-suffering Olga radiates a soothing note and prefers to avoid confrontation (ineffectually remonstrating with Natasha at the start of Act III and hiding behind the screens later in that act to protect herself from Masha's candour), Masha's personality is altogether more spiky, uncomfortable, and unpredictable. When Vershinin is called away in Act II, she rounds on both Anfisa and Chebutykin, prompting Natasha to reproach her (pretentiously, in French) for having 'rather coarse manners'. Just before her Act III 'confession', Olga actually rebukes her sister: 'Masha, you're silly. You're the silliest person in our family...'[23] Masha has a certain devil-may-care quality, quite unlike the prudent, and possibly slightly prudish, Olga. In this, perhaps, she shows herself as the general's daughter.[24]

The youngest sister, Irina, experiences the greatest change within the play. When the curtain rises, on her twentieth birthday, she has an air of such innocence (like Nina at the start of *The Seagull* or Anya in *The Cherry Orchard*). She longs naively for love, and work, and happiness, and a blissful return to Moscow – and, act by act, as the years pass, we see her face age and her hopes sag, as prose proves stronger than poetry and the real ousts the ideal. At times, Irina comes close to despair, especially in the third act, when she has forgotten the Italian for 'window' and 'ceiling', and feels she is sinking into a kind of abyss. By the end of the play, she regains some of her lost poise, but she will never know such innocence again.

The fourth member of the Prozorov family is the most marginal, Andrei. Not only is he excluded from the title of the play, but by nature he chooses to hover in the wings, never seeking centre-stage. As the sole male heir of a presumably 'successful' general, he is burdened with excessively high hopes – above all, that he might become a professor at Moscow University, and so provide his sisters with a ticket to paradise. Shy and retiring by disposition, Andrei might seem to manifest a steady going to seed, with his journey a downward spiral, as the physical conquers the spiritual. He puts on weight as soon as his father dies,[25] and then plunges into a disastrous

23 In contrast, Chekhov had suggested to Olga Knipper (in his letter of 21 January [3 February] 1901) that, as Masha, Knipper should seek to convey at the end of Act III that 'you're cleverer than your sisters, or at least that you regard yourself as cleverer'.

24 When rehearsing the role of Masha, Olga Knipper wrote to Chekhov on 13 December 1900: 'Mariya Petrovna [Lilina, the first Natasha] has decided that I'm the spitting image of Daddy [the General], Irina – Mummy, while Andrei has his father's face and his mother's character...'.

25 Andrei tends to be weak-willed, and was clearly overshadowed, and even dominated, by his father. In Act I, when Irina declares that 'Father was a soldier, but his son chose an academic career', Masha significantly adds:

marriage, followed by gambling, the mortgaging of the family house,[26] and the acceptance of a humiliating place on the local council run by his wife's lover. And yet, beneath the increasingly piggish exterior, beats the tortured mind of an indomitable idealist. Andrei's speeches throughout the play, especially his virtual monologues in the presence of the deaf Ferapont, convey the bitterness of disillusionment and an intensity of yearning.

A somewhat perplexing figure within the family circle is Masha's husband, the Latin teacher, Kulygin. This pedantic, unimaginative man may appear instantly ridiculous, or even loathsome – a kind of blood-brother to the Greek teacher, Belikov, in Chekhov's story, *The Man in a Case* (*Chelovek v futliare*) (1898). Masha noticeably recoils from such an unromantic spouse. Kulygin seems to be an antique fossil,[27] purveyor of a dead language (and dead marriage?), walking in awe of his tedious headmaster and aspiring to no more than a schoolboy's humour. Yet, as the play progresses, our perception of Kulygin may change. His undeniable limitations are the reverse side of his virtues – he is a dull but kindly man, who has the misfortune to love his unloving wife, and to be hurt by her unfaithfulness. Kulygin conceals his genuine grief behind Latin tags and a borrowed beard.

In his letter to Olga Knipper on 15 September 1900 Chekhov referred to the play's 'four important female roles, four educated young women'. If knowledge of a foreign language may be loosely equated with 'education', then the odious Natasha may lay claim to being 'educated'. On several occasions she readily mangles the French tongue, as if to underline her stupendous insensitivity.[28] Andrei's wife is unutterably vulgar, a discarder

---

'Which was what Father wanted.' On his first entry Andrei admits that their late father 'oppressed' them with education, making them all learn several languages.

26 Masha remarks angrily in Act III: 'He's mortgaged this house to the bank and his wife has grabbed all the money. But the house doesn't belong just to him – it belongs to all four of us!'

27 Kulygin's actual age is not given. The actor Alexander Vishnevsky, for whom the part was written, was born in 1861 and therefore about forty years old at the time of the Moscow première. The first draft of Act IV contains some lines (excluded from the final version) which suggest that Kulygin is still fairly young, and was once blissfully in love with Masha. Kulygin recalled: 'When I was Masha's fiancé, I used to wander around just like a madman, like a drunkard... I was beside myself with happiness...' (XIII, 298). Natasha's age is also unknown. Presumably she is in her early twenties, although she seems decidedly less innocent and childlike than Irina.

28 In contrast, none of the linguistically proficient Prozorovs ever utters a non-Russian word, except when Masha mockingly conjugates the Latin verb 'to love' in Act III.

of 'useless' old women (Act III), and destroyer of beautiful trees (Act IV),[29] who regards violin-playing as 'sawing' or 'scraping' and rages at the sight of a misplaced fork (Act IV). Natasha plays a crucial role in the drama, through shaping the action and serving as a contrast to Andrei and his sisters. She may be seen as a ruthless usurper, invincibly vindictive and petty – or (more dubiously) as a positive agent of competitive enterprise. Natasha's activity has to be evaluated against the background of wider themes, such as love, happiness, and meaning. The dramatist never exaggerates her vileness, even if she reveals herself as the incarnation of *poshlost'*.[30]

Two men closely connected with Masha and Irina act also as the play's main 'philosophers'. Lieutenant-Colonel Vershinin is a profoundly ambiguous figure, both as lover and as visionary. On one level, he might appear as a traditional romantic hero, the sophisticated stranger from Moscow, sporting smart military uniform and exuding eloquent charm. His growing intimacy with Masha is perhaps central to the 'love plot', and his orations raise one's thoughts to the future destiny of mankind.[31] Yet Vershinin is long past the rosy flush of youth (in Act I he is already forty-two), and displays a certain flabbiness of mind and body. A hostile critic might simply conclude that he talks too much and falls in love too easily.

The other 'philosopher', Baron Tuzenbakh, is less compromised or controversial. Unlike the middle-aged Vershinin, Tuzenbakh is 'not yet thirty' (Act I), and nor is he burdened by a suicidal second wife. His chief characteristics include a dogged devotion to Irina and an ever-readiness to join Vershinin in speculative jousts. Alas, the 'Germanic' Baron is blessed with the gift of ugliness, and his love proves unrequited. Good-natured and totally without guile, Tuzenbakh is inspired by a naive longing for hard work and marital bliss.

The Baron's arch-tormentor (apart from cruel fate) is his colleague and rival, the mysteriously menacing Captain Solyony. This would-be Lermontovian clone may appear manically possessed – he harbours a dark desire for Irina, and agonises awkwardly in any social situation. Solyony is not a monster or a stage villain (he may be overridingly shy, as he hints to Tuzenbakh in Act II), and yet he is thoroughly destructive. In the course of

---

29 Unlike Natasha, Chekhov himself planted trees, and looked after the former family cook – even his last letter to his sister Masha on 28 June (11 July) 1904 conveys greetings to 'Grannie', M.D. Belenovskaya.

30 *Poshlost'* embodies all that is vulgar, common, trivial, trite, banal and contentedly second-rate, poisoning the air with its complacent round of falsehood and deceit.

31 Moreover, Vershinin's arrival in Act I, and departure in Act IV, promotes the symmetry of the action.

the play, he gradually deprives the hapless Tuzenbakh of everything – first (Act II), of chocolates to eat, and then (Act IV), of a last cup of coffee, the prospect of marriage, and life itself.

There is usually one doctor in Dr Chekhov's plays, although, as ever, one should beware of identifying the character with the author. The army doctor, Chebutykin, is sixty years old (Act II) and close to retirement (Act IV). At first he seems a grandfatherly figure, benign and slightly eccentric, doting on Irina and imparting useless pieces of information, culled from endless newspapers.[32] Yet, increasingly, a sense of self-disgust takes control of Chebutykin, an acute awareness of his wasted life and squandered knowledge. Like Dr Astrov in *Uncle Vanya*, he recalls a patient who recently died (Act III),[33] and, like Astrov, he resorts to alcohol for solace. Chebutykin had been devoted to the three sisters' mother, and his essential loneliness breeds in him an ever deepening indifference or callousness. The apparently benevolent prankster of Act I gives way to the malign nihilist of Act IV.

The remaining four characters in *Three Sisters* are more self-contained and less intrinsic to the plot, although they certainly reinforce the impression of an ensemble. The former nurse Anfisa, aged eighty-one by Act III, is one of those faithful old retainers haunting Chekhov's last three plays. Anfisa lacks, however, the idiosyncratic convictions or comic quirkiness of Marina (in *Uncle Vanya*) and Firs (in *The Cherry Orchard*) – she is a pathetic victim of Natasha's malice rather than the embodiment of an entire *ancien régime*.

Her counterpart from outside the family walls is deaf old Ferapont, another long-suffering labourer representing Russia's lower orders. Ferapont features unforgettably in scenes with Andrei, pestering him with official papers and prompting impassioned outpourings of grief. These tragi-comic non-exchanges are among the most painful in the play, and are often cited as extreme examples of Chekhovian 'non-communication'.

In his letter to Maxim Gorky on 16 October 1900, Chekhov had remarked that, in *Three Sisters*, 'the milieu consists of soldiers, artillery...'. Of the nine male characters listed in the *dramatis personae* only three (Andrei, Kulygin

---

32 Chekhov may have derived this latter trait from his own recently deceased father. In a letter to his brother Alexander on 21 March 1892 he had remarked: 'Father likes philosophising as in days of yore, posing questions such as: Why is snow lying there? Or: Why are the trees over there, and not here? He reads newspapers all the time...'.

33 A difference, however, is that Chebutykin feels culpably negligent: 'I've forgotten everything I knew, I don't remember a thing... And it's my fault that she died. Yes...'. As a practising doctor, Chekhov himself had frequently dealt with death. Thus, in a letter of 12 May 1893 he observed: 'A female patient of mine died today of consumption...'.

and Ferapont) are civilians from the outset.[34] Most of the men tend to be somewhat staid – even in moments of jollification, such figures as Kulygin, Vershinin, Chebutykin, Andrei and Solyony scarcely radiate dynamic exuberance. Accordingly, the two youthful second lieutenants, Fedotik and Rodé, perform a useful, if minor, dramatic function by enlivening the action at various points. Rather like Tweedledum and Tweedledee (or Bobchinsky and Dobchinsky in Gogol's *The Government Inspector* [*Revizor*]), Fedotik and Rodé usually act as a duo and may appear to have virtually interchangeable personalities. Fedotik freezes the fleeting moment by taking photographs at the end of Act I and start of Act IV, and also poignantly spins a humming-top at Irina's birthday party.[35] In Act II both men sing quietly to a guitar accompaniment. Fedotik and Rodé seem hardly more than schoolboys,[36] whom time has not yet touched. Even when the Act III fire destroys most of his possessions, Fedotik merely laughs at the strangeness of it all.

The world of *Three Sisters* is not, however, exhausted by these fourteen listed characters.[37] Two unnamed officers (evidently not Fedotik and Rodé) enter at the very end of Act I, to behold the 'kissing couple' (Chekhov's stage direction). A housemaid helps Anfisa to clear the table and put out the lights late in Act II, before informing Natasha of Protopopov's arrival.[38] The stage direction at the start of Act IV states that passers-by occasionally cross the garden on their way to the river, and 'half a dozen [literally, about five] soldiers march briskly past'. Later, Solyony is seen in the distance, accompanied by 'two officers'. The Act IV farewells are briefly interrupted by the appearance on stage of two itinerant musicians, a man and a girl, who play a violin and harp. Vershinin, Olga and Anfisa listen to them for a while in silence, before Anfisa (at Olga's bidding) gives them money and sends them on their way. Anfisa comments explicitly on the people's misery: 'You wouldn't

---

34 Lieutenant Tuzenbakh eventually opts for civilian life, before the start of Act III.

35 Chekhov does not actually specify that the humming-top should be spun. The stage direction merely indicates that Fedotik takes the top out of his pocket, whereupon he comments 'It makes a wonderful sound' and Irina replies 'How delightful!' In most productions, however, the top is spun on the floor and everyone listens with rapt attention to its mysterious, magical sound.

36 Indeed, Rodé teaches gymnastics at the high school (Act I).

37 The cast list in the play's first publication (*Russkaia mysl'* 2 [1901]) concluded with the words: Officers, Servants.

38 In Act III, when justifying her ejection of Anfisa, Natasha declares that she already has a dry-nurse and a wet-nurse, and that the family has a housemaid and a cook. The dry-nurse is heard singing, off-stage in Act II.

have to busk on a well-fed stomach'.[39] On another occasion, late in Act II, the voices and laughter of the long-awaited mummers are heard off-stage, before Anfisa is dispatched to bar their entry.

There are also several 'invisible' characters whose presence is felt throughout the play. The Prozorov children frequently recall their dead mother and father, to whom they owe their life and education, while Chebutykin maintains his unswerving devotion to the memory of their mother. If the dead parents are largely symbols of the past (which continues to affect the present), other unseen figures remain very much alive. The pernicious Protopopov moves ever closer to the centre of the action, progressing from the seemingly remote menace of Act I to the almost tangible intruder of Act IV, lurking on the other side of the wall, within the Prozorovs' house. Natasha cloyingly dotes on her two infants, Bobik and Sofochka (baby Bobik is sitting up in his pram as the final curtain falls),[40] while Vershinin repeatedly refers to his suicidal wife and his two unfortunate daughters. A tragi-comic shadow is cast by Kulygin's busy headmaster, who blights Masha's life while appearing to Kulygin as a shining beacon.[41]

---

39 This belated intrusion of two strangers, followed by Anfisa's sociological generalisation, is perhaps the only awkward excrescence in the entire play. (An analogous instance occurs late in Act II of *The Cherry Orchard*, with the appearance of the tipsy passer-by.) The reader or audience is well aware of Russia's poverty and backwardness from other speeches in the play – actually to show a beggar or two on-stage seems a superfluous piece of raw 'realism', untypical of the dramatist (see his comment about the nose in Kramskoy's painting, quoted in *Literaturnoe nasledstvo*, LXVIII: *Chekhov* [Moscow, 1960], p. 418). However, one critic offers a perceptive justification for this episode in *Three Sisters*, which may be interpreted as 'a symbol of banished music' (where music represents 'beauty, the fullness of life, love') – see E.M. Sakharova, in *Chekhoviana: Chekhov v kul'ture XX veka* (Moscow, 1993), pp. 77-8.

40 Bobik thus 'appears' on-stage, although in actual productions he usually remains unseen within his pram.

41 Many other figures are mentioned in passing. Thus, in Act II Irina tells of the woman who wished to send a telegram after the death of her son, and early in Act III Olga alludes to the 'Kolotilin girls' (or 'young ladies') sheltering downstairs. In Act IV Kulygin recalls his school-friend Kozyrev ('*ut consecutivum*'), and Chebutykin identifies an off-stage call as coming from Skvortsov, the second in the duel. In Act III the doctor guiltily remembers a female patient who died 'last Wednesday'. The deaf Ferapont parades an array of eccentrics (such as the pancake-guzzling merchants) in his colourful anecdotes about Moscow. In one sense, the number of unseen people hovering over the play is almost infinite – from all the pupils of the past fifty years listed in Kulygin's book (Act I), and the 'hundred thousand inhabitants' of the

Three Sisters may also be regarded as a tale of two cities, the ideal and the real. Ever-beckoning, yet tantalisingly out of reach, lies Moscow (Mecca, Eden,[42] demi-paradise), cradle of a golden childhood, font of future happiness. Meanwhile, those who yearn for Moscow must dwell in 'a provincial town such as Perm' (as Chekhov himself wrote in his letter of 16 October 1900). When the dramatist visited that actual city (situated some 700 miles east of Moscow), he recoiled in horror: 'Life here near Perm is grey and uninteresting, and if one were to portray it in a play, it would be too oppressive...' (letter of 25 June 1902). In Act IV of *Three Sisters* Andrei delivers a devastating indictment of the 100,000 local inhabitants. Moscow and the 'provincial town such as Perm' coexist in constant tension, as two opposing characters throughout the drama.[43]

The Themes

In a perfect world, perhaps, there would be no loneliness, illness, disappointment, and death.[44] Moscow and the 'town such as Perm' might be superseded by another city, 'the new Jerusalem', where 'there will be no more death, and no more mourning or sadness'.[45] In *Three Sisters*, however, Chekhov portrays the real world, and not the heavenly city. His characters

---

provincial town, evoked by Andrei in Act IV, to the remote 'descendants of my descendants' imagined by Vershinin in Act II.

42 *Three Sisters* might also be considered a 'tale of two gardens'. In Act IV, which is set outside, in the old garden belonging to the Prozorovs' house, Tuzenbakh remarks: 'What beautiful trees, and really, what a beautiful life there should be all around them!' In a way, Chekhov's more sensitive characters yearn for the garden of Eden (*sad Edemskii*, Genesis 2:15, 3:23), paradise lost. In Act II of *The Cherry Orchard* (more literally, *The Cherry Garden* [*Vishnevyi sad*]), Trofimov declares: 'All Russia is our orchard' (or garden [*Vsia Rossiia nash sad*]).

43 Of Chekhov's great quartet, *Three Sisters* is the only piece which is set in a town (rather than on a landowner's estate). Yet this difference scarcely alters the atmosphere of the play, and Act IV is set outdoors, in the garden.

44 Chekhov would probably have agreed here regarding loneliness – 'loneliness is the lousiest of feelings' (letter of 13 August 1889). A notebook contains the striking words: 'As I shall lie alone in my grave, so in essence I live all alone' (XVII, 86). Concerning death he was remarkably stoical – 'I personally do not fear even death or blindness...' (letter of 25 November 1892). However, A.S. Suvorin's diary for July 1897 records these thoughts of Chekhov about death: 'Death is cruel, a repulsive punishment... It's terrible to become nothing. People will carry you off to the cemetery, return home, and then drink tea and make hypocritical speeches. It's repugnant to think about that...' (*Dnevnik A.S. Suvorina* [Moscow-Petrograd, 1923], p. 165).

45 The Book of Revelation 21:1-4 (from *The Jerusalem Bible*).

mourn and grieve, and he offers no solution to their suffering. Yet what might appear merely depressing can be truly inspiriting, for despite his claim to the contrary in his letter of 25 November 1892, Chekhov belonged to the 'best' type of 'realistic' writer:

> Remember that the writers we call eternal or merely good, and who intoxicate us, possess one extremely important feature in common: they are going somewhere and summon you to follow them, and you can sense with your entire being, not only with your mind, that they have a definite aim... The best writers among them are realistic and describe life as it is, but because every line is saturated with a conscious aim, you can feel, apart from life as it is, also life as it should be, and this captivates you...

In *Three Sisters*, the burden of sorrow and non-achievement is balanced, and even perhaps transcended, by the yearning for happiness and fulfilment. The portrayal of life as it is engenders a longing for life as it should be.

Nearly all the characters in *Three Sisters* (as in *The Seagull* and *Uncle Vanya*) are discontented with their present existence. This widespread 'mood' or feeling fuels the subsequent dramatic action, and implicitly disproves the notion that Chekhovian characters are 'passive' or 'inert'. Their unhappiness prompts them to *seek* happiness – they do not retreat into spiritual or emotional torpor.[46] Yet whether they seek wisely may remain a matter for debate.

Love

Perhaps no other area of human life promises so much and delivers so little as the prospect of romantic or sexual love.[47] When writing *The Seagull*, Chekhov had noted with some amusement: 'It's a comedy, with three female roles, six male, four acts, a landscape (a view of a lake), much talk about

---

46 In this respect, the 'yearning' (and hence vulnerable) characters in *Three Sisters* would support the Tartar's defiant assertion (in Chekhov's story of 1892, *In Exile* [*V ssylke*]): 'God created man so that he should be alive, so that there should be joy and longing and grief, but you want nothing, so you're not alive, but a stone, mere clay!...'.

47 In one of his notebooks Chekhov wrote: 'Love. It is either a remnant of something that is degenerating and that once was vast, or it is a part of that which in the future will develop into something vast, but in the present it does not satisfy, it gives much less than you hope' (XVII, 77).

literature, little action and five tons of love...' (letter of 21 October 1895). Nearly everyone in that play is caught in a chain of unrequited love – Medvedenko pursues Masha who pines for Konstantin who adores Nina who worships Trigorin (who prefers fishing); Arkadina also clings to Trigorin, while Polina sighs for Dorn (who is fully sated).

It is a feature, both comic and sad, of Chekhov's major plays that love is seldom returned, and marriages soon fall flat. The near-inevitability of failure in love may make the effort appear absurd. Certainly, the dramatist conveys a keen sense of irony, as the blind follow the blind, chasing the phantom of love and marital bliss. Yet such ironic awareness need not be equated with cynicism – Dr Chekhov himself was not above the human herd, perusing his creations from some detached Olympian height. He too was susceptible to the lure of love.

Chekhov's life and letters provide ample evidence of his attitude to women, love, sex and marriage. While admitting to several discreet affairs (letters of 24 or 25 November 1888 and 21 January 1895), as well as casual couplings (letters of 27 June and 9 December 1890), he persistently sought to protect his freedom, as man and writer, from the encroachment of marriage:

> I don't want to get married, and there's no one in the offing. And to heck with it, anyway. I'd be bored, saddled with a wife. But I wouldn't mind falling in love. Life is boring without a powerful love...
>
> (*To A.S. Suvorin*, 18 October 1892)

> All right, I'll get married if you insist. But these are my conditions: everything must remain as it was before, that is, she must live in Moscow and I in the country, and I shall visit her. I couldn't abide a happiness which continues day in, day out, from one morning to the next... I promise to be a splendid husband, but give me a wife who, like the moon, does not appear every day on my horizon. N.B. Getting married won't make me a better writer...
>
> (*To A.S. Suvorin*, 23 March 1895)

Chekhov first set eyes on Olga Knipper on 9 September 1898, and they became lovers in July 1900. Marriage loomed ahead. On 25 May 1901 (less than four months after the première of *Three Sisters*), their wedding took place in Moscow. The forty-one-year-old writer had barely three more years to live, during much of which time he languished in Yalta, while his wife acted in Moscow. Yet, despite misunderstandings and occasional strain, the marriage seems to have suited Chekhov:

> This marriage hasn't altered in any respect either my way of life or the way of life of those who lived and still live close to me. Everything, absolutely everything, will remain as it was, and as before I shall continue to live in Yalta alone...[48]
>
> (*To his sister Masha*, 4 June 1901)

> I got married two or three years ago and I'm very glad; I think my life has changed for the better. The things people usually write about married life are absolute nonsense...
>
> (*To V.L. Kign* [*Dedlov*], 10 November 1903)

In *Three Sisters* the dramatist – himself about to take the plunge after years of resolute bachelorhood – depicts three unhappy marriages.[49] The first concerns Masha and Kulygin, who seem so patently mismatched. In Act II Masha remarks to Vershinin: 'I was married [off] when I was eighteen, and I was afraid of my husband, because he was a teacher and I had hardly left school. He struck me then as terribly learned, clever and important. That's no longer the case, alas...'. When the curtain rises, Masha is about twenty-two,[50] and thoroughly bored after four years of marriage. Unlike her expansive sisters, Masha appears introverted – cloaked in black and deliberately discordant (reading, whistling, then declaiming the mysterious opening lines of Pushkin's *Ruslan and Lyudmila* [*Ruslan i Liudmila*]). Everything about her husband and his work annoys Masha – his slavish emulation of the headmaster, the organised outings for the teachers and their families, those tedious evenings at the headmaster's (Act I), and, no doubt, the very sound of Kulygin's voice. Love for her has hardened into habit ('I'm used to him', Act II). When yet again he reiterates his love (Act III), her response cruelly parodies his endless Latin tags by offering the arid conjugation of the Latin verb 'to love': *'Amo, amas, amat, amamus, amatis, amant'*.[51]

---

48 Thus Chekhov fulfilled his prophecy of 23 March 1895.

49 By contrast, his last play *The Cherry Orchard* – the only piece he wrote as a married man – virtually avoids the portrayal of marriage. All the characters in his closing comedy are unmarried.

50 Whereas Act I conveys the information that Olga is twenty-eight and Irina twenty, Masha's age has to be calculated by indirect means. Chekhov places her second among the sisters in the cast list. In Act III Irina is twenty-three, and Kulygin indicates that he has been married to Masha 'for seven years'. Accordingly, Masha (who married at eighteen) must be about twenty-five in Act III, some two years older than Irina. Andrei's age is also never given, but somehow the 'weight' of his character would suggest that he comes second of the four Prozorov children, between Olga and Masha.

51 In the first of his Latin mottoes it may appear that Kulygin almost delivers his

Her husband, Fyodor Ilyich Kulygin, first enters the play as a kind of walking advertisement against marriage. Towards the end of Act I, as soon as Vershinin has expressed his own (and, the audience already senses, also Masha's) sentiment about wedlock – 'If I could start my life again, I wouldn't get married... No, no!' – Kulygin strides on stage, wearing his teacher's uniform and spouting in his placid, stilted way. He means no harm, but brings no joy. For much of the action, it might be held that Kulygin is totally insensitive to his wife's feelings – in Act I, after tidily noting that the carpets should be put away till winter, he slides his arm round Masha's waist, laughs, and in one breath asserts: 'Masha loves me. My wife loves me. And the curtains will have to be put away as well, together with the carpets...'. Throughout the play Kulygin remains a figure of fun, in his awful pedantry (rather as Epikhodov in *The Cherry Orchard* is a perpetual comic disaster). Yet Kulygin is not a caricature. His horizons may be limited, but he loves his wife with a beatific dedication, and becomes increasingly perturbed by her many absences in Acts II and III ('Where's Masha?' ['*Gde Masha*?']) and distressed by her grief at another man's departure (Act IV). Unfortunately, his faithfulness to his marriage vows spells further doom for Masha – as Vershinin exits for ever, the embarrassed Kulygin attempts to console his wife: 'My good Masha, my kind Masha... You are my wife, and I'm happy come what may... I'm not complaining, not reproaching you at all... Olya here's my witness... We'll start our life all over again in the same old way, and I shan't say a word to you, not a hint...'. Olya (Olga) is his 'witness' – and she could have been his wife. In a moment of insight, early in Act III, Kulygin had observed: 'My dear Olechka... I often think: if it weren't for Masha, I'd have married you, Olechka... You are very kind...'. Indeed, Kulygin and Olga might have made a fitting match – two 'dull' and faithful teachers. Alas, the human heart is rarely wise.[52]

In her Act II comment to Vershinin – 'I was married [off] when I was eighteen' ('*Menia vydali zamuzh, kogda mne bylo vosemnadtsat' let*') – Masha seems

---

wife, by displacement, to Vershinin. He presents Irina with the boring book he has written (a history of his school), remarking: '*Feci quod potui, faciant meliora potentes*' ('I've done what I could – let those who can, do better') – words traditionally spoken by Roman consuls upon ceding power to their successors (XIII, 465). When Irina points out that Kulygin had already given her a copy for Easter, the undaunted Kulygin transfers the book to Vershinin.

52 By Act IV, Kulygin evidently realises that he might also have been happier with Irina. He remarks (as if forlornly trying to convince himself): 'Irina's a very nice girl. She's even a bit like Masha, always wrapped up in her own thoughts. But you, Irina, have a gentler disposition. Although Masha has a very nice disposition, too. I love her, I love my Masha'.

almost to be disclaiming responsibility for her poor choice of spouse. Yet presumably she was not forced into marriage, and a moralist may condemn her rejection of her husband and her subsequent adultery with Vershinin. The relationship between Masha and Vershinin appears central to the love-plot, since it blossoms and dies entirely within the framework of the play. Although it is tempting to invest their love with the tragic pathos of traditional romance, such a clichéd approach would vulgarise their actual liaison. Masha is no *femme fatale*, oozing languorous sensuality, and Vershinin is no dashing hero, trailing clouds of glory. The reality is more ordinary and much sadder. In her Act III 'confession', Masha charts the progress of her emotions:

> I love Vershinin... At first I found him strange, then I felt sorry for him...and then I grew to love him... I grew to love him with his voice, his words, his misfortunes and his two little girls... I love him – so that's my fate... And he loves me... It's very frightening, isn't it? It's not good?... When you read some novel or other, it all seems so trite and obvious, but when you fall in love yourself, you see that no one knows anything and everyone must decide for himself...

Lieutenant-Colonel Vershinin is an enigmatic 'hero'. He enters in Act I, and declares his love for Masha early in Act II. Throughout the third act he and Masha communicate merely by means of a love-call:

MASHA. Tram-tam-tam...
VERSHININ. Tram-tam...[53]
MASHA. Tra-ra-ra?
VERSHININ. Tra-ta-ta. (*He laughs.*)[54]

---

53 In some editions: Tam-tam...

54 This private language between Masha and Vershinin has been much discussed. According to Nemirovich-Danchenko, when asked to explain its meaning during the first reading of the play, Chekhov replied that it was 'nothing in particular', 'just a joke' (foreword to: Nikolai Efros, *'Tri sestry': P'esa A.P. Chekhova v postanovke Moskovskogo Khudozhestvennogo teatra* [Petersburg, 1919], p. 8). In a letter to Olga Knipper on 20 January (2 February) 1901, Chekhov wrote: 'Vershinin pronounces "tram-tram-tram" by way of a question, and you – by way of an answer...'.

This coded language could signify that Masha and Vershinin are about to become lovers. Olga Knipper (rehearsing as Masha) wrote to Chekhov on 26 January 1901: 'I've decided that by means of "tram-tam"... she says that she loves him and will give herself to him (*i budet prinadlezhat' emu*), i.e. a declaration which he has long been seeking... After all, until that night their

Towards the end of that act, Masha admits to her sisters that she loves Vershinin, before exiting in response to his off-stage summons of 'Tram-tam-tam!' (to which she loudly replies: 'Tra-ta-ta!'). Finally, in a short scene late in Act IV, they part as lovers.[55]

Chekhov signals subtly the first hints of mutual attraction, from Vershinin's initial 'I seem to remember *your* face a little' (and Masha's teasing reply 'But I don't remember you!')[56] to her demonstrative removal of her hat – 'I'm staying for lunch' – after his enthusiastic 'philosophical' speech. Since there is a vacuum in the lives of both Masha and Vershinin, it is scarcely surprising that they turn to one another for comfort. What is puzzling, however, is the nature of Vershinin's romantic attachment. When Tuzenbakh first mentions the imminent arrival of the new battery commander and Irina asks whether he is an 'interesting' man, Tuzenbakh replies:

> He's all right, but he's got a wife, a mother-in-law, and two little girls. What's more, this is his second marriage. He goes round calling on people, announcing everywhere that he has a wife and two little girls. He'll tell you about it, too. His wife's a bit half-witted, with a long girlish plait, she talks in a highfalutin way,

---

relationship has been pure [or chaste, *chistye*], hasn't it?...' Stanislavsky (rehearsing as Vershinin) noted at this point in his production score (p. 215): 'To be acted as if Masha asks him: "Do you love me?" Vershinin replies: "Yes, very much". Masha: "Today I shall be yours (*Segodnia ia budu prinadlezhat' tebe*)". Vershinin: "Oh, happiness, oh, joy"'. If so, then Masha and Vershinin were to become lovers some three years after their first meeting. The amorous use of 'tra-ta-ta' is said to have a real-life basis, in a conversation witnessed by Chekhov in 1896 (see XIII, 423-4).

55 In Acts I and II Masha and Vershinin address one another by the formal pronoun *vy* (you, corresponding to the French *vous*, etc.). The 'love-call' in Act III avoids the use of a personal pronoun, although Vershinin's laughter and Masha's 'confession' perhaps suggest the complicity of intimacy (actual or imminent). During their Act IV farewell, they openly employ the intimate, second-person singular form (cf. the French *tu*), reflected in the verbal endings (*proshchai*, *pishi*, *ne zabyvai*, *pusti*). A similar transition from *vy* to *ty*, revealing their new status as lovers, is apparent in Chekhov's own correspondence with Olga Knipper from 9 August 1900 onwards.

In Act IV Irina and Tuzenbakh also address one another as *ty* (having previously been on *vy* terms) – but in this case the pronoun *ty* merely reflects their legitimate status as an engaged couple, and carries no implication of sexual intimacy.

56 Though a few moments later Masha does remember him as 'the lovesick major' in Moscow.

> philosophising,[57] and every so often she tries to commit suicide, apparently just to annoy her husband. I'd have left a woman like that long ago, but he puts up with it and just keeps on complaining...

Attempted suicide and marital strife are deadly serious topics, and yet they are placed here in a somewhat ludicrous context. To be predictably self-repeating may be risible, and accordingly the audience laughs when Vershinin duly obliges later in Act I:

> I have a wife and two little girls, what's more my wife is in poor health and so on and so forth, but if I could start my life again, I wouldn't get married... No, no!

Early in Act II, he expatiates upon his latest domestic trials to Masha, and wonders why Russian husbands and wives torment and plague one another. He even claims: 'I never talk about these things, and it's strange, I complain to no one but you...'. He then kisses her hand and, a few lines later, avows his love for Masha.

Vershinin's propensity for romance may border on the comic. In Act I he is already forty-two ('Oh, how much older you look!', exclaims Masha, candidly).[58] At least eleven years earlier, when the sisters were still in Moscow, he was known as 'the lovesick major'. Now, two marriages on, he turns his attention to Masha. Although nothing in the play (no self-indicting soliloquies or snide remarks from others) casts doubt upon the sincerity of his sentiments for Masha, the suspicion yet remains that for Vershinin, perhaps, both love and talk are shallow pastimes. He departs with his brigade, leaving behind a disconsolately sobbing mistress and a suicidal second wife. (His first wife's fate is unexplained – perhaps she managed to commit suicide?)[59] Such imputations may

---

57 *Filosofstvuet* – a trait she shares with Vershinin.

58 As one critic observes: 'Vershinin, who knew the girls (and their father) many years before in Moscow...is twenty years older than Masha, almost a father figure' (Albert Bermel, *Contradictory Characters* [New York, 1973], p. 77).

59 Preparatory notes for the play reveal that Chekhov originally intended Masha to attempt suicide (apparently, in Act III). The notes read: 'In Act III Irina: you don't do anything! Masha: I've tried to poison myself! (*ia otravilas'!*)'; 'Kul[ygin], upon learning that Masha has tried to poison herself, is above all afraid lest they find out about it at school' (XVII, 214). Presumably Kulygin was afraid of upsetting his headmaster. This episode, which was not incorporated in the final text, would have shown Kulygin in an uncommonly heartless light. It might also have suggested a bizarre parallel between Masha

seem harsh, for Chekhov's stage direction in Act IV indicates that Vershinin is 'deeply moved' (*rastrogannyi*) as he abandons Masha.[60] Both lovers may have accepted the impermanence of their affair, and yet, though he urges Masha not to forget him, it seems doubtful that he will remember her for long.[61] A hostile viewer might maintain that, in Vershinin, grand passion is reduced to an amorous itch. More fairly, it might be felt that he is an ordinary, unheroic mortal, readily susceptible to the blandishments of love. Peggy Ashcroft, who took part in the illustrious 1938 production of *Three Sisters*, later observed: 'Vershinin is a windbag, without very much heart. I think he's a bit of a ladykiller, and Masha suffers at his hands...'.[62]

The third unhappy marriage involves Andrei and Natasha. Their union seems foredoomed, and bliss lasts a mere instant. Those who marry rashly have time to repent. Andrei breathlessly blurts out his love at the end of Act I, and (as if a moment later) has no more words to say by the beginning of Act II. His reasons for marrying may appear ambiguous. At the simplest level, he hopes for happiness. Late in Act III he declares: 'When I got married I thought we would be happy...we'd all be happy... But oh my God!...' – and he weeps. A shy man such as Andrei can easily fall for the tinsel beauty of Natasha. There is no definite proof that hidden motives underlie his hasty proposal, such as a desire to escape from the burden of his sisters' (and his late father's) expectations. Andrei does not seek mediocrity and defeat.

His sisters, however, spurn Natasha from the outset. Their attitude might seem condescending and even cattish, as both Masha and Olga recoil from her vulgarity and lack of taste.[63] Certainly, Olga is tactless in Act I, when

---

and Vershinin's wife – in Act II Vershinin observes phlegmatically: 'My wife has again tried to poison herself (*otravilas'*)...'.

60 As Turgenev had noted, however, in Chapter IX of his novel *Rudin* (1856), 'no one is as easily carried away by his emotions [or, no one falls in love as easily] as a dispassionate man (*nikto tak legko ne uvlekaetsia, kak besstrastnye liudi*)'.

61 One commentator remarks: 'Despite his charm, and the ringing optimism of his "philosophising", the last word on Vershinin is not Masha's, but rather his own request to Olga, to watch over his emotional left luggage for a month or two, until he's settled into the next garrison town, with doubtless another flower-filled room in the offing...' (Stephen Mulrine, introducing his translation of *Three Sisters* [London, 1994], p. xvi).

62 Peggy Ashcroft's words on 5 January 1989, quoted in *Chekhov on the British Stage*, edited by Patrick Miles (Cambridge, 1993), p. 86.

63 Originally Chekhov intended that, while attempting to defend Natasha towards

she draws attention to Natasha's unbecoming green belt.[64] Yet the sisters are justified in dreading Natasha's intrusion into the family. They are conscious of her close involvement with Protopopov, which continues throughout the play. Masha asserts in Act I: 'I heard yesterday that she's going to marry Protopopov, the chairman of the local council. An excellent idea!...'

As Natasha takes over the house, Andrei retreats into gambling and gloomy silence, punctuated by occasional impassioned outbursts. He becomes profoundly disillusioned with his wife, and pronounces (Act IV) the most devastating indictment of her awfulness:

> My wife is – my wife. She's honest, decent, and – yes – she's kind, and yet at the same time there's something about her which reduces her to the level of a petty, blind, rough-skinned animal. At all events she's not a human being... I love Natasha, it's true, but sometimes she strikes me as amazingly vulgar, and then I grow confused and can't understand why, for what reason I love her so or, at least, used to love her...

After hearing these words, Chebutykin advises Andrei to abandon Natasha and to wander off (like a tramp), without looking back: 'And the further you go, the better.' A benevolent onlooker will fervently hope that Andrei might heed this advice.

In the course of the play, Natasha produces two children – Bobik by Act II, and Sofochka by Act III. Although she drools over her offspring, she manifestly uses them as pawns to advance her domestic control. It may well be that Protopopov is Sofochka's natural father – Act II ends with Natasha's departure for a tryst with the local chairman, and by the beginning of Act III baby Sofochka has appeared.[65] One shudders to imagine the future of such progeny, under Natasha's malign sway. Even though children 'rank with the angels' (as Chekhov claimed in a letter of 2 January 1889),

---

the end of Act III, Andrei should condemn his sisters as capricious 'old maids': 'Old maids don't like their sisters-in-law, and never have liked them – that's always the case' (XIII, 296).

64 And Natasha duly claims her revenge in Act IV, by damning Irina's 'tasteless' belt.

65 A further clue to Sofochka's paternity is provided in Act IV. Natasha (who in Act III had declared: 'I like order in the house!') seems to pair her children off with their respective fathers: 'Protopopov...will sit with Sofochka, and Andrei...can push Bobik's pram'.

audiences rightly relish Solyony's Act II riposte to Natasha's maternal prattle: 'If that child were mine, I'd fry him in a frying-pan and eat him.'

It seems probable that *Three Sisters* chronicles the course of two adulterous affairs. One may censure both liaisons equally (according to the absolute Commandment, 'Thou shalt not commit adultery'), or refrain from condemning either (following the biblical 'He that is without sin among you, let him first cast a stone at her').[66] If, however, one applies relative moral criteria, the cases of Masha and Natasha merit separate evaluation. Masha entered into matrimony in good faith, although unwisely, before drifting into infidelity after several unsatisfying years. Natasha, in contrast, embarked upon marriage already laden with the encumbrance of a likely lover, and probably perpetuated this liaison throughout the days of her marriage. Whereas the Masha-Vershinin relationship seems sad, the Natasha-Protopopov affair is merely sordid.

There is a fourth marriage hovering above the action, about which only vague conjectures are possible. The three sisters and their brother often recall their dead parents. Were General Prozorov and his wife blissfully wed? In almost every act of the play Chebutykin remembers his love for the mother of the Prozorov children. Late in Act II he converses with Andrei:

> CHEBUTYKIN. I never got round to marrying, because my life flashed by like lightning, and also because I was madly in love with your dear mother, and she was married already...
> ANDREI. There's no point in marrying. No point, because it's boring.
> CHEBUTYKIN. That may be so, but what about loneliness? You can philosophise as much as you like, but loneliness is a terrible thing...[67]

Eventually, in Act IV, an enigmatic exchange takes place:

> MASHA. Were you in love with my mother?
> CHEBUTYKIN. Very much so.

66 John 8:7 (Authorised King James Version). Unless otherwise indicated, all biblical quotations are taken from this translation.

67 Ironically, one of Chekhov's notebooks contains the thought: 'If you're afraid of loneliness, then don't get married' (more precisely: 'don't take a wife' [*ne zhenites'*]) (XVII, 85).

MASHA. And did she love you?
CHEBUTYKIN (*after a pause*). That I no longer remember.

There is a possibility (but nothing is certain) that Chebutykin may be Irina's father.[68] He is particularly attached to Irina, showering her with endearments. In Act I he calls her 'my little girl, my joy' (*devochka moia, radost' moia*):

CHEBUTYKIN. (*To Irina.*) My darling, my dear little child (*Milaia, detochka moia*), I've known you since the day you were born... I carried you in my arms... I loved your mother, God rest her soul...[69]
IRINA. But why such expensive presents?[70]

Significantly, after these lines Stanislavsky noted in his production score (p. 101): 'Bear in mind that, according to a statement by the author, Irina (probably) is the daughter of Chebutykin, who lived with her mother'.

In Act II Chebutykin tells Irina: 'I can't do without you'. This emotional need perhaps helps to explain why he drops and breaks her mother's clock in Act III, shortly after hearing that Irina might soon go away (he may wish to 'stop time'?), and why he remains in such imperturbable good humour throughout the final act, in which he assists at the duel which kills Irina's fiancé (although, at the end, Irina still intends to leave alone).

Chebutykin is 'nearly sixty' when the play begins, and was therefore nearly forty when Irina was born. Could it be that the story of Masha and Vershinin echoes a saga of twenty years earlier?

Despite the abundant evidence of marital misery, several unmarried characters in *Three Sisters* aspire to wedded bliss.[71] In the context of Chekhov's

---

68 At the end of Act I Chebutykin describes himself, half-jokingly, as 'an old sinner' where love is concerned. The possibility of concealed paternity arises also in *The Seagull* – it seems that an early version of that play explicitly identified Dr Dorn as Masha's father.

69 Lines in the first draft of this speech hinted at Chebutykin's near-suicidal loneliness: 'If it wasn't for you [that is, the three sisters], I would probably already have taken to drink, or simply put a bullet in my own head...' (XIII, 276). This was replaced in the final version by: 'If it wasn't for you, I'd have departed this life long ago...'.

70 Chebutykin had just presented Irina with a silver samovar.

71 Only the peripheral characters remain untouched by love – the aged Anfisa and Ferapont, and the youthful Fedotik and Rodé. True, Fedotik showers Irina with presents – flowers and perhaps the humming-top in Act I, coloured

play, their natural yearnings may appear slightly absurd. When the curtain rises, with the only married sister gloomily clad in black, Olga is undeterred: 'All is well, everything comes from God, and yet it seems to me that if I got married and stayed at home all day, then that would be better.' She pauses and (as if unconsciously rebuking Masha?) adds: 'I would love my husband.' At this point, in a separate conversation elsewhere on-stage, Tuzenbakh remarks to Solyony: 'You talk such nonsense, I'm tired of listening to you.' The play contains numerous instances of such ironical undercutting, where the interweaving of unrelated conversations or the juxtaposition of contrasting psychological states opens up unexpected and enticing vistas. Irony notwithstanding, Olga remains a poignant emblem of emotional unfulfilment. Rather like Sonya in *Uncle Vanya*, or Varya in *The Cherry Orchard*, she is one of the plain but pure in heart, condemned to perpetual frustration.

Whereas Olga regards marriage as a duty, Irina pursues the dream of love. Late in Act III Olga advises her youngest sister to marry the ugly, but decent, Baron:

> OLGA. After all, we don't marry for love, but merely to fulfil our duty. That's what I think, anyway, and I would marry without love. I'd marry anyone who proposed to me, as long as he was a decent person. I'd even marry an old man...
> IRINA. I kept on waiting for us to move to Moscow, and there I should meet my real one, I dreamt of him and loved him... But it's proved to be all nonsense, all nonsense...

Because she is waiting for her ideal 'real one' ('*moi nastoiashchii*') Irina is unmoved by her actual suitors. She declines the patiently devoted Tuzenbakh late in Act I, and ejects the menacingly insistent Solyony late in Act II. Although, with a mixture of desperation and resignation, she eventually accepts the kindly Baron, their final parting in Act IV is profoundly elegiac:

> TUZENBAKH. I'll take you away tomorrow, we shall work, we'll be rich, my dreams will come true. You will be happy.

---

crayons and a penknife in Act II, and (but for the fire) a little notebook in Act III. Yet such prodigality seems a comically endearing characteristic of the schoolboyish Fedotik, rather than a sign of amorous attachment to Irina. Fedotik simply enjoys giving presents to children – at the end of Act II, when he learns that Bobik is ill, he immediately promises: 'I'll bring him some nice little toy tomorrow...'. Departing from the play in Act IV, he bestows a notebook and pencil upon Kulygin.

> But there's just one thing, one thing: you don't love me!
> IRINA. That's not in my power! I shall be your wife, faithful and obedient, but I feel no love, and that's how it is! (*She weeps.*) I've never been in love in all my life. Oh, I've had such dreams of love, I've been dreaming for a long time, night and day, but my soul is like an expensive piano, which is locked and the key is lost.
> *Pause.*
> Your eyes are restless.
> TUZENBAKH. I lay awake all night. There's nothing so terrible in my life that could really frighten me, but that lost key torments my soul and will not let me sleep. Say something to me.
> *Pause.*
> Say something to me...
> IRINA. What? What? All around everything is so mysterious, the old trees stand and are silent... (*She rests her head on his chest.*)[72]
> TUZENBAKH. Say something to me.
> IRINA. What? What am I to say? What?
> TUZENBAKH. Anything.
> IRINA. That's enough! Enough!
> *Pause.*

Irina is too honest to lie, to cast a crumb of comfort before the Baron departs to his death. One critic harshly claims that 'Irina is remarkably unpleasant to both her suitors'.[73] In contrast, Peggy Ashcroft (who in 1938 played Irina to Michael Redgrave's Tuzenbakh) looked back with sympathy upon the characters and the performance:

> Michael Redgrave as the Baron was one of his finest performances ever... He created this bumbling, plain, shy, talkative, not-meaning-anything character. He's *intensely* lovable, and Irina *wants* to love him, but she can't really...[74]

---

72 Irina's words 'All around everything is so mysterious, the old trees stand and are silent', and the stage direction (*She rests her head on his chest*), have been restored in XIII, 180, on the basis of Chekhov's earlier versions. Apart from their quality of poetic tenderness, they strengthen two leitmotifs of the play, and especially of Act IV: trees, and a sense of mystery. The concept of mystery (*taina*), mysteriousness (*tainstvennost'*), pervades the final act.

73 Laurence Senelick, *Anton Chekhov* (London, 1985), p. 110.

74 Peggy Ashcroft's words on 5 January 1989, quoted in *Chekhov on the British*

Tuzenbakh perishes as a helpless victim of the darkly vengeful Solyony.[75]

No firm conclusions can be drawn about Chekhov's attitude to love and marriage. Although he himself warned against the crass identification of his own views with those of his characters (letter of 23 October 1902), it is perhaps tempting to look for clues in his story *About Love* (*O liubvi*) (1898). There the protagonist, Alekhin, offers several observations:

> So far only one incontestable truth has been uttered about love – namely, that 'this is a great mystery'...[76] The best thing, in my opinion, is to explain each case separately, without making any attempt to generalise. One ought, as doctors say, to individualise each particular case...
>
> When you love, in your reasonings about that love you must proceed from what is highest, from what is more important than happiness or unhappiness, sin or virtue in their accepted meaning, or you must not reason at all...

Work

Despite the prominence of its love-theme, *Three Sisters* is not primarily a play about love. Its characters do not spend all their time mooning about the stage, suffering from *chagrin d'amour*. In the quest for fulfilment, work also plays a significant role.

According to popular misconception, the typical character in a Chekhov play is an effete representative of Russia's privileged élite, given to vacuous conversation over endless cups of tea. Since *Three Sisters* and *The Cherry Orchard* are set at the turn of the century, a politically-minded reader or audience might feel predisposed to view the action (or inaction) as foreshadowing the revolutions of 1917. References to work, especially to *trud*

Stage (Cambridge, 1993), p. 86.

75 It is not fully clear whether Solyony (whose third duel this is) definitely intended him to die. At the end of Act II he had sworn 'by all that's holy' to 'kill' any successful rival, and yet shortly before the duel he claimed: 'I'll just wing him like a woodcock'. The timing of the duel (the day before Tuzenbakh's marriage to Irina) suggests that Solyony has planned a desperately pointless act of annihilation. Early in Act I he casually threatened to 'put a bullet' through Chebutykin's head, although, by displacement, this threat almost appears directed against Tuzenbakh, who has just spoken.

76 A biblical echo – see Ephesians 5:32.

(labour, perhaps hard physical work), may be seized upon to seek to demonstrate the dramatist's supposed political sympathies.

Towards the end of Act I, Irina might seem to lend support for a sociological approach when she declares:

> We must work, just work. The reason we are melancholy and take such a gloomy view of life is that we've not experienced real work. We are the children of people who despised work...

The most ardent encomium to *trud* occurs earlier in Act I, from the lips of Irina and Tuzenbakh:

> IRINA. When I woke up this morning, and got up and washed, I suddenly felt I understood everything in this world, and I knew how to live. Dear Ivan Romanych, I understand everything. Man must labour and work by the sweat of his brow, whoever he may be, and here lies the meaning and aim of his life, his happiness and delight. How wonderful to be a workman who gets up at dawn and breaks stones on the road, or a shepherd, or a teacher who teaches children, or an engine-driver on the railway... Good heavens, never mind being human – one would rather be an ox or a simple horse, providing one *worked*, than a young woman who rises at noon, then drinks coffee in bed, then takes two hours to dress... Oh, that's dreadful! You know the way one sometimes longs for a drink on a hot day – that's the way I suddenly longed to work. And if I don't start getting up early and working really hard, then stop being my friend, Ivan Romanych.
>
> CHEBUTYKIN (*tenderly*). I'll stop, I'll stop.
>
> OLGA. Father taught us to get up at seven o'clock. Now Irina wakes up at seven and lies in bed till at least nine, pondering upon something or other. And with such a serious expression on her face! (*She laughs.*)
>
> IRINA. You still treat me like a little girl and think it's strange when I look serious. I'm twenty years old!
>
> TUZENBAKH. This yearning for work, heavens, how well I understand it! I've not done a stroke of work in my entire life. I was born in Petersburg, that cold, idle place, in a family which had never known work or worry. I remember how I used to come home from cadet school and act like a spoilt child while the servant was pulling off my boots, and my mother would gaze at me dotingly, and feel amazed if others took a different view. They tried to protect me from hard

> work. But they haven't quite succeeded, not quite! The time has come, a great cloud is descending upon us, a healthy mighty storm is brewing, it's on the move and is already near, and soon it will blow away from our society all the laziness, indifference, the prejudice against work, the rot of boredom. I shall work and, twenty-five or thirty years from now, everyone will work. Everyone!
> CHEBUTYKIN. I shan't work.
> TUZENBAKH. You don't count...

As so often in Chekhov's plays, the above passage is serious and profoundly comic. Both Irina and Tuzenbakh are naive, and patently ignorant concerning the reality of hard work. Irina proclaims: 'How wonderful to be a workman who gets up at dawn and breaks stones on the road, or a shepherd, or a teacher who teaches children...' – and yet she herself lies in bed till at least nine, and seems not to have heeded the agonised speech, a few minutes earlier, of her teacher-sister Olga, who is exhausted after four years of toil ('I've felt my strength and youth leaving me every day, drop by drop...'). As for Tuzenbakh, he may loyally echo his beloved's ingenuous yearning for work, yet his lifelong avoidance of labour scarcely qualifies him as a social prophet ('a healthy mighty storm is brewing...').

Without actually rising at dawn to break stones on the road, Irina does rouse herself to sample various jobs – but reality proves a sobering experience. She becomes exhausted and irritated by 'soulless, mindless' work at the post office (Act II – '*trud bez poezii, bez myslei*', more literally 'work without poetry, without even thinking'), and reaches the frontiers of despair in Act III:

> I can't work, I won't work. I've had enough! I used to be at the post office, and now I work for the town council and I loathe and despise everything they give me to do... I'm already twenty-three, I've been working for ages, and my brain has dried up, I've grown thin and ugly and old, and I've nothing, nothing, no satisfaction, and time is passing and I feel I'm going further away from a real, beautiful life, ever further and further, towards some abyss...

Albeit even more urgently (for we remember the radiant Irina of Act I), she is repeating her sister Olga's path, down the *via dolorosa* of job dissatisfaction.[77]

---

77 But for Tuzenbakh's untimely death, Irina would also have emulated her sister Masha, by accepting a husband she did not love.

And, indeed, by the end of the play, she is about to follow Olga into the teaching profession, although one hopes her eyes are now more open to 'reality':

> We must go on working, just working! Tomorrow I'll leave alone, I shall teach at the school and devote my entire life to those who may need it. It's autumn now, winter will soon be here, covering everything with snow, but I shall work, I shall work...

In the quest for more meaningful employment Baron Tuzenbakh resigns from the army, before Solyony's bullet finally robs him of Irina, and his cup of coffee – and the opportunity to start work at a brick-works.[78]

Three Sisters is not a play *about* work or the 'working class' (unlike, for instance, Gorky's *Enemies* of 1906). Chekhov's characters are presented at moments of leisure and recreation – attending a birthday party or looking forward to a Shrovetide celebration, unwinding after a fire or saying their final farewells. It would be mistaken, however, to imagine that they are idle and without occupation. Olga works all-too-hard as a teacher, and Kulygin is all-too-preoccupied with his headmaster's school. (By Act IV, as a parallel to Olga's promotion, Kulygin's pedagogic zeal has raised him to the rank of second master or deputy head [*inspektor*].)[79] Andrei toils for the county council, even if this activity seems less exalted than the coveted rank of professor.[80]

In his letter of 16 October 1900 Chekhov remarked that 'the milieu consists of soldiers, artillery'. The six soldiers he portrays seem a generally amiable bunch, ranging from the boyish Fedotik and Rodé to the loquacious

---

78 Tuzenbakh had been thinking 'for five years' of resigning his commission (Act II), and early in Act III he appears, wearing new and fashionable civilian clothes. Later in the same act, Olga admits that she wept when she first saw him in a civilian coat – 'he looked so plain [or ugly, *nekrasivym*]'. One critic comments on the work aspirations of Irina and Tuzenbakh: 'The issue is real, the solution false: What could a dreamy schoolgirl and a philosophical Baron contribute to a brickworks?' (Howard Moss, in *The Hudson Review*, XXX, 4 [Winter 1977-8], p. 538). Innokenty Annensky assumes that Tuzenbakh intended to work there as a book-keeper or accountant (*bukhgalter*) – see his *Kniga otrazhenii* (St Petersburg, 1906), p. 150.

79 Chekhov had a good, first-hand knowledge of schools and schoolteachers. His brother Ivan and sister Masha were both teachers; in 1896-9 he had supervised the construction of three schools (in Talezh, Novoselki and Melikhovo); and in Yalta he became a governor of the girls' high school.

80 Not that Chekhov had any illusions about the essential eminence of professors. Serebryakov in *Uncle Vanya* typifies professorial pomposity and pseudo-scholarship.

Vershinin and Tuzenbakh.[81] Admittedly, this company rarely radiates military zeal – one may note with some alarm that Doctor Chebutykin has forgotten everything he once knew (Act III), and that Tuzenbakh as yet has never 'done a stroke of work' (Act I). Nevertheless, Masha pays a handsome tribute to the troops in Act II ('Perhaps it's different elsewhere, but in our town the most decent, the most noble and cultivated people are the military...'),[82] and Vershinin in Act III is delighted with his men's response to the fire ('If it hadn't been for the soldiers the whole town would have gone up in flames. Splendid fellows!'). Tuzenbakh observes in Act III that, if the brigade moves on, 'the town will be quite deserted', and Irina in Act IV uses the same two words (*gorod opusteet*) to denote the abandoned town.[83]

Stanislavsky takes pains to emphasise Chekhov's benevolence towards the military:

> There had been rumors that he had written a play against the army, and these had aroused confusion, expectation, and bad feelings on the part of military men. In truth, Anton Pavlovich always had the best of opinion about military men, especially those in active service, for they, in his own words, were to a certain extent the bearers of a cultural mission, since, coming into the farthest corners of the provinces, they brought with them new demands on life, knowledge, art, happiness, and joy. Chekhov least of all desired to hurt the self-esteem of the military men.[84]

The more enlightened characters in *Three Sisters* seek the elusive ideal of satisfying work. (Natasha, in contrast, does not work – she merely manoeuvres and schemes.)

---

81 Solyony, however, cannot help being destructive, and Chebutykin becomes increasingly uncaring.

82 Of course, Masha's comment may, in part, be regarded as a compliment to Vershinin – she is disenchanted with her civilian husband and beginning to warm to the Lieutenant-Colonel.

83 The image of emptiness and desertion is also conveyed by Andrei in Act IV: 'The town will be deserted (*Opusteet gorod*)'; 'Our house will be deserted (*Opusteet nash dom*)'.

84 Constantin Stanislavsky, *My Life in Art* (London, 1924), p. 374. Stanislavsky also states that, when going abroad in December 1900, Chekhov deputed a 'lovable colonel' (V.A. Petrov) to supervise rehearsals in his absence, 'to see that there should be no mistakes made in the customs of military life, in the manner and method of the officers' bearing in the play, in the details of their uniforms, and so on' (ibid., p. 374).

Although he frequently professed a streak of south Russian indolence, Anton Chekhov devoted his short life to literary, medical and philanthropic work. And, like many active men, he yearned for the luxury of idleness.

On 20 July 1901 – a few months after the première of *Three Sisters* – a medical colleague, M.A. Chlenov, wrote to Chekhov that he (Chlenov) would never experience 'personal happiness', and so would work instead 'on behalf of science and general ideas'. In his reply four days later Chekhov maintained: 'To work on behalf of science and general ideas – that's what personal happiness is...'.

As writer and as doctor, without clamouring for acclaim, Chekhov knew the quiet satisfaction of a life of modest, dedicated work.

Happiness

Three Sisters is a play about happiness, or about the elusiveness of happiness. Human beings may pursue many goals in life – power, fame, success, money. Chekhov's characters yearn for happiness. The longing for love and satisfying work forms part of this wider quest, as does the search for meaning and, perhaps, God. That the grail proves tantalisingly out of reach is both dispiriting and uplifting.

The words 'happiness' (*schast'e*) and 'happy' (*schastlivyi*) reverberate throughout the play, for, at various times, many of the characters feel a temporary joy, or contentment, or even happiness.[85] Thus, at the start of Act I, both Olga and Irina refer to the 'joy' (*radost'*) they experienced on that May morning, and Chebutykin uses the same word to address Irina (*radost' moia* – 'my darling', literally 'my joy'). Upon his first entry, Kulygin declares himself to be 'cheerful' (*vesel*) and 'happy' (*chuvstvuiu sebia schastlivym*) on this Sunday, a day of rest, and for much of the play he claims that he is 'contented' (*dovolen*, Acts III and IV)[86] and even 'happy'

---

85 Chekhov's characters tend to be emotionally volatile – they readily laugh, smile, weep, sob, and fear. Masha often feels angry, and Andrei – embarrassed. Exceptions are the unsmiling Solyony (seeking to maintain his fierce Lermontovian pose) and the vulgar Natasha (who, apart from moments of genuine petty rage, seems to simulate larger authentic emotions such as anxiety, moral outrage, and perhaps embarrassment). Several characters express themselves at times 'through tears' (*skvoz' slezy*). Chekhov explained this phrase later, in connection with *The Cherry Orchard* (letter of 23 October 1903): 'I often use the stage direction "through tears", but that's meant to indicate merely the character's mood, and not real tears'.

86 This gives rise to a comically brutal exchange of triplets between Masha and Kulygin in Act III. When Kulygin exclaims: 'I'm contented, contented,

(*schastliv*, Act IV). Solyony blurts out the words 'Oh, happiness!' (*O schast'e!*) upon declaring his love for Irina in Act II, and, when spurned, instantly threatens: 'But there must be no happy rivals of mine...' (*schastlivykh sopernikov*, 'happy' or 'successful' rivals). Masha in Act IV addresses the birds flying overhead as 'my happy ones' (*schastlivye moi*) and wishes the departing soldiers a 'happy journey' (*Schastlivyi im put'!*).

Alas, in practice, few of Chekhov's characters are granted a 'happy journey'. By Act II, the workworn Irina seems to Tuzenbakh like an 'unhappy' dear little child (*takoi malen'koi, neschastnen'koi*), and in Act III she laments: 'Oh, I'm unhappy...' (*O, ia neschastnaia...*). In Act IV, shortly before her final parting with Vershinin, Masha recognises: 'When you have to take happiness (*schast'e*) in little snatches, in little pieces, and then lose it, as I have, you gradually become coarsened and foul-tempered...' By Act IV the professedly 'contented' Kulygin can no longer maintain a spurious façade. Throughout the play he has tried to convince himself and others that his wife is 'good' or 'kind', until eventually he has to confess:

> No matter what they say, Masha is a good, upstanding woman, I love her very much and I'm thankful for my lot... People have different lots in life... There's a certain Kozyrev who works in the excise office here. He was at school with me, but he got expelled from the fifth form because he simply couldn't grasp the *ut consecutivum*.[87] He's dreadfully hard up now, and in poor health, and whenever I happen to meet him I always say: 'Hello, *ut consecutivum!*' Yes, he says, quite so, *consecutivum*, and he gives a cough... Whereas I've been lucky all my life, I'm happy (*ia schastliv*), I even have the Order of St Stanislav second class, and now I myself teach others this same *ut consecutivum*. Of course, I'm a clever man, cleverer than many others, but that's not the same as happiness (*no schast'e ne v etom*)...

At such moments, the ridiculous-seeming Kulygin strikes a note of genuine pathos. Indeed, his disappointment late in Act II over the cancellation of

---

contented!' (*Ia dovolen, ia dovolen, ia dovolen!*), Masha retorts: 'And I'm bored, bored, bored...' [or 'And I'm fed up, fed up, fed up...'] (*Nadoelo, nadoelo, nadoelo...*).

87 A syntactical construction in Latin.

the Shrovetide party, although couched in comic terms, might be said to encapsulate the mood of the entire play: '*O, fallacem hominum spem!*'[88] Always the accusative for exclamations...'.

The fullest discussion of happiness in the play occurs during the Act II 'philosophical' debates involving, in particular, Vershinin and Tuzenbakh. In the evening twilight characters muse and ponder:

> VERSHININ. Oh well, if we can't have any tea, let's at least have a bit of philosophising.
> TUZENBAKH. By all means. What about?
> VERSHININ. What about? Let's dream...for instance, of life as it shall be after we are gone, in two or three hundred years' time.
> TUZENBAKH. Very well then. After we are gone, people will fly around in air balloons, the cut of their coats will be different, perhaps they'll discover a sixth sense and develop it, but life itself won't change – a life which is difficult, and full of mystery, and happy (*schastlivaia*). And a thousand years from now man will still be sighing: 'Ah, how hard life is!' – and yet, just as now, he will be afraid of death and unwilling to die.
> VERSHININ (*after a moment's thought*). Well, how shall I put it? It seems to me that everything on earth is bound to change gradually, and is already changing before our very eyes. In two or three hundred years, or even a thousand – the precise time doesn't matter – a new happy life will dawn (*nastanet novaia, schastlivaia zhizn'*). Of course, we shall have no part in it, but it's the reason for our living now, and our working, and, yes, our suffering, we are creating that life – and this alone is the purpose of our existence and, if you

---

88 'Oh, illusory hope(s) of men!' Kulygin sprinkles Latin phrases throughout the play, underlining his ludicrous pedantry as the local Latin teacher – *Feci quod potui, faciant meliora potentes*; *mens sana in corpore sano* (Act I); *o, fallacem hominum spem!* (Act II); *In vino veritas*; *Omnia mea mecum porto* (Act III); *modus vivendi*; *ut consecutivum* (Act IV). It might be noted, however, that Dr Chekhov liked sprinkling his own correspondence with Latin expressions – 'I wish *tibi optimum et maximum*' (July [?] 1875); 'On 11-12 October I am moving and *omnia mea mecum porto* to Yakimanka, Lebedeva's house' (6-8 October 1885); 'They need *mens sana in corpore sano*' (March 1886). Chekhov had written Cicero's phrase '*O fallacem hominum spem!*' at the top of his letter to M.M. Kovalevsky on 8 (20) January 1898.

like, our happiness (*nashe schast'e*).

Masha laughs quietly.

TUZENBAKH. What's the matter?

MASHA. I don't know. I've been laughing all day.

VERSHININ. I went to the same cadet school as you, I didn't go on to military academy; I do a lot of reading, but I'm not much good at choosing my books, and perhaps I read all the wrong things, and yet the longer I live, the more I want to know. My hair is turning grey, I'm nearly an old man already, and yet I know so little, oh so little! But it seems to me that I do know, and know for sure, the most important and the most essential thing. And I wish I could make you see that for us there can be no happiness, there must not and shall not be (*chto schast'ia net, ne dolzhno byt' i ne budet dlia nas*)... All we must do is work and work, whereas happiness is the lot of our remote descendants (*a schast'e – eto udel nashikh dalekikh potomkov*).

Pause.

If not for me, then at least let it be for the descendants of my descendants.

Fedotik and Rodé appear in the ballroom; they sit down and sing quietly, one of them strumming on a guitar.

TUZENBAKH. So, according to you, we may not even dream of happiness! But what if I *am* happy?!

VERSHININ. You're not.

TUZENBAKH (*throwing up his arms and laughing*). We clearly fail to understand one another. Now how can I convince you?

Masha laughs quietly.

(*Holding up a finger to her.*) Laugh at that then. (*To Vershinin.*) Not merely in two or three hundred years, but even a million years from now life will remain exactly the same; life doesn't change, it remains constant, following its own laws which are none of our concern or which, at least, we'll never fathom. Migrating birds,[89]

89 Birds figure frequently in the imagery of *Three Sisters* (as well as providing a central symbol in *The Seagull*). Early in Act I Irina links the idea of happiness with 'great white birds' overhead, whereupon Chebutykin addresses her tenderly as 'my white bird'. In Act II Vershinin remarks upon the birds which the French minister noticed only from his cell window. Here, in Act II, Tuzenbakh refers to the 'migrating' or 'migratory' birds, the 'birds of passage'

the cranes,[90] for instance, just fly and fly, and no matter what thoughts, great or small, may flit across their minds, they will still go on flying, without knowing where or why. They fly and will go on flying no matter what philosophers may spring up in their midst; and let them philosophise as much as they like, as long as they keep on flying...

MASHA. But isn't there any meaning?

TUZENBAKH. Meaning?... It's snowing outside. What's the meaning of that?

Pause.

MASHA. It seems to me that man must have faith or seek faith, for otherwise his life is empty, empty... How can you live and not know why the cranes fly, why children are born, why there are stars in the sky... Either you know why you live, or everything's pointless, mere straw in the wind.

Pause.

VERSHININ. All the same, it's sad one's youth has gone...

MASHA. Gogol said: living on this earth is a bore, my friends![91]

TUZENBAKH. And I'll say: arguing with you is a chore, my friends! Oh really, I give up.

CHEBUTYKIN (*reading a newspaper*). Balzac was married in Berdichev...[92]

(*pereletnye ptitsy*), such as cranes – and in Act IV this image is reprised by Chebutykin (who feels he has been left behind like a bird [*pereletnaia ptitsa*] which is now too old to fly away with the flock) and – more significantly – by Masha (who perhaps links the sight of birds literally flying overhead with the departing soldiers, including Vershinin, and the overall transience of human life): 'The migrating birds are already on the wing... Swans or geese... My dear ones, my happy ones (*schastlivye moi*)...'.

90 Some ten years earlier, Chekhov would willingly have accompanied the cranes: 'Autumn is in the air. And yet I love the Russian autumn. It has something remarkably sad about it, and welcoming, and beautiful. I'd love to fly off somewhere with the cranes...' (letter of 29 July 1891). From about 1900, one or two tame cranes lived at Chekhov's Yalta *dacha*.

91 Masha has added the word *zhit'* (to live) to the famous last line of Gogol's *The Story of how Ivan Ivanovich Quarrelled with Ivan Nikiforovich* (*Povest' o tom, kak possorilsia Ivan Ivanovich s Ivanom Nikiforovichem*) (1835).

92 The French novelist Honoré de Balzac (1799-1850) married his mistress, Countess Hanska (whom he had known since 1833) in the Ukrainian town of Berdichev on 14 March 1850. Since the writer was already mortally ill, and died five months later, his marriage can scarcely be regarded as a cloudless

A few minutes later, the theme of happiness resumes:

> MASHA. Happy the man who (*Schastliv tot, kto*) doesn't notice whether it's winter or summer. It seems to me that, if I were living in Moscow, I shouldn't care about the weather...
> VERSHININ. The other day I was reading the diary of some French cabinet minister, which he wrote while in prison. The minister was sentenced for the Panama affair. With what rapture and delight he speaks of the birds which he can see from his prison window and which he hadn't noticed before, when he was still a minister.[93] Now, of course, that he's free once more, he again fails to notice those birds. And in the same way, you won't notice Moscow when you're actually living there. Happiness is not for us and never shall be, we merely long for happiness.
> TUZENBAKH (*picking up a box from the table*). What's happened to the chocolates?
> IRINA. Solyony's eaten them up.
> TUZENBAKH. All of them?...

The above sections touch upon many of the play's themes, while reflecting subtle fluctuations of mood. The characters in *Three Sisters* often say silly things – after all, as Chekhov himself wrote in a letter of 18 January 1886: 'It's tedious to be clever all your life...'. And yet, amid the irrelevances and inanities of everyday conversation and behaviour, these characters reach out towards the great questions: happiness, time, meaning, faith. They are vulnerable beings, trembling on the brink of nothingness. Hence Chekhov's reported advice:

> Everything on stage should be just as complex and also just as simple as in life. People eat their dinner, just eat their dinner, yet at the same time their happiness is taking shape and their lives are being smashed...[94]

---

event. Various commentators have sought profound symbolic significance in these words, which Chebutykin pronounces twice and Irina 'pensively' or 'dreamily' echoes. Much more convincingly, Nils Åke Nilsson views this episode as a rhythmical contrast, without any specific 'hidden meaning' (in *Anton Čechov: 1860-1960. Some Essays*, edited by T. Eekman [Leiden, 1960], pp. 176-7).

93 See Ch. Baïhot, *Impressions cellulaires* (Paris, 1898), p. 18 (according to XIII, 465).

94 Chekhov's words spoken in 1889, as recalled by I.Ia. Gurliand in *Teatr i iskusstvo* 28 (11 July 1904), p. 521.

The development of the action might appear to confirm people's view that the 'mood' of *Three Sisters* is 'gloomier than gloom itself' (from Chekhov's letter of 13 November 1900). When the play ends, most of the characters seem further away from happiness than they were at the beginning. Ironically, the only 'happy' person in Act IV is the aged Anfisa, who now has a room of her own to live in (or die in?): 'I sometimes wake up at night and – O Lord, dear Mother of God, I'm the happiest person in the world! (*schastlivei menia cheloveka netu!* – literally, there's no one happier than I am!)'.[95] Yet it should also be remembered that the play is suffused with comedy, and does not end in despair. As the curtain falls, the sisters speak of their determination to live, and Olga predicts that 'happiness (*schast'e*) and peace' will reign upon earth.

Recurrent themes in Chekhov's works suggest that the writer was deeply conscious of the near-impossibility and even undesirability of 'personal happiness' (with its element of narrow selfishness).[96] In a letter to his sister Masha on 13 November 1898, shortly after his father's death, he made one of his most eloquent pronouncements:

> Tell Mother that... come what may, winter must follow summer, old age follow youth, after good fortune comes misfortune and vice versa; man cannot be healthy and happy all life long, losses always attend him, he cannot elude death, even be he Alexander the Great – and one must be ready for everything and look upon everything as inevitable and necessary, no matter how sad this may be. All one must do to the best of one's ability is fulfil one's duty – and that's all...

---

95 Natasha, who might seem to triumph by Act IV, is capable of experiencing satisfaction rather than happiness.

96 Personal happiness is shown as an illusion in *The Russian Master* (*Uchitel' slovesnosti*) (1894), and the desire for personal happiness appears trivial in *Gooseberries* (*Kryzhovnik*) (1898) and immoral in *On Official Business* (*Po delam sluzhby*) (1899). Unhappiness, too, is egoistic in *Enemies* (*Vragi*) (1887). In *Gooseberries* Ivan Ivanych suggests that outside the door of every contented or happy person someone should stand tapping with a little hammer to remind the happy that unhappy people exist and that, sooner or later, life will show its claws, and illness, poverty or bereavement will strike. One of Chekhov's notebooks contains the thought: 'How unbearable at times are people who are happy and always successful!' (XVII, 93).

Moscow

Languishing in their provincial exile, the Prozorovs long for Moscow, their native city and scene of their happy childhood. The non-departure for Moscow is perhaps the main non-event of the play.

In her second speech in Act I, Olga informs Irina (and the audience, for there is much exposition in Act I) that they left Moscow eleven years ago. As she speaks, Tuzenbakh, Chebutykin and Solyony are standing behind some columns, conducting their own separate conversation:

> OLGA. Eleven years have gone by, yet I remember everything there as if we'd left only yesterday. Heavens, how wonderful! I woke up this morning, and saw a blaze of light, I saw the springtime, and joy stirred in my heart, I felt a passionate longing to go home.
> CHEBUTYKIN. The devil you did!
> TUZENBAKH. It's nonsense, of course (*Konechno, vzdor*).
> *Masha, brooding over a book, softly whistles a tune.*
> OLGA. Don't whistle, Masha. How could you!
> *Pause.*
> Because I spend every day at school and then give lessons until evening, I have a perpetual headache and the thoughts of an old woman. And indeed, these four years I've been working at the high school, I've felt my strength and youth leaving me every day, drop by drop. And only one thing grows and gets stronger, one dream...
> IRINA. To go to Moscow. To sell our house, finish with everything here, and then to Moscow...
> OLGA. Yes! As soon as we can – to Moscow.
> *Chebutykin and Tuzenbakh laugh.*
> IRINA. Our brother will probably be a professor, so he won't want to live here anyway. Poor Masha's our only problem.
> OLGA. Masha will come to Moscow every year, for the entire summer.
> *Masha softly whistles a tune.*
> IRINA. God willing, it will all turn out as we hope...

The emotional affinity of Olga and Irina is reflected in their shared longing for Moscow, as Irina completes Olga's sentence ('one dream...'/'To go to Moscow...'). At the same time, Masha strikes a discordant note, and the ironically overlapping conversation of the military men effectively foredooms their 'passionate longing' ('The devil you did!'/'It's nonsense, of course'/ *Chebutykin and Tuzenbakh laugh*). One senses also Irina's religious or fatalistic passivity – 'God willing, it will all turn out as we hope' ('*Bog dast, vsë ustroitsia*').

Throughout the play, the departure for Moscow is steadily postponed. In Act I, in May, on her twentieth birthday, Irina claims: 'We hope to be there by autumn...'. Some twenty-one months later, in Act II, she declares: 'Dear Lord, I dream of Moscow every night, I'm like some madwoman. (*She laughs.*) We're moving there in June, so that leaves...February, March, April, May...nearly half a year!' By Act III, when she is already twenty-three, Irina sobs:

> We shall never go to Moscow... I can see that we won't go... I kept on waiting for us to move to Moscow, and there I should meet my real one, I dreamt of him and loved him... But it's proved to be all nonsense, all nonsense (*No okazalos', vsë vzdor, vsë vzdor*)...

Unconsciously, Irina confirms here Tuzenbakh's oblique pronouncement in Act I ('It's nonsense, of course') – both characters employ the word *vzdor*. Nevertheless, just as Act II had ended with Irina's plaintive triple cadence ('Moscow! Moscow! Moscow!' ['*V Moskvu! V Moskvu! V Moskvu!*' – literally, 'To Moscow! To Moscow! To Moscow!']), so Act III concludes with Irina beseeching her eldest sister:

> Let's go to Moscow! I implore you, let's go! There's no place on earth better than Moscow! Let's go, Olya! Let's go!
> *Curtain.*

For the Prozorovs, Moscow represents perfection. If Irina considers her home town the best place on earth, so Olga remembers May in Moscow as all blossom, warmth and sunshine (Act I), Andrei dreams every night of being a famous professor at Moscow University, and would gladly shake off provincial loneliness by dining, alone, in a huge Moscow restaurant (Act II), while Masha feels that in Moscow she would be happy, and therefore not care about the weather (Act II).

This vision of Moscow does not remain unchallenged within the play. For the Prozorovs, one of the initial attractions (Act I) of Vershinin is that he comes from Moscow – yet he consistently rejects any idealised picture of that city. Vershinin indicates that Moscow does not mean automatic happiness,[97] and in Act I expresses a preference for the local scene (with its

97 Hence his words to Masha in Act II: 'You won't notice Moscow when you're

'healthy', 'Russian' climate, and its 'wide' and 'wonderful' river), so unlike the 'gloomy bridge' in Moscow near which a solitary person feels sad.

Meanwhile, the deaf and ancient Ferapont provides a grotesque running commentary, portraying Moscow as a bizarre realm where a merchant may eat forty or fifty pancakes and then die, and across which a gigantic rope is stretched (telegraph wires?, Act II), and offering an idiosyncratic historical analogy to the Act III fire: 'Moscow went up in flames as well, back in 1812. Goodness gracious me! Weren't the French surprised!'[98] By Act IV the benighted messenger is unable to distinguish Petersburg from Moscow:

> The porter at the revenue office was telling me just now... He reckoned that last winter there were a frost in Petersburg of two hundred degrees... He reckoned two thousand people froze to death. Scared stiff they were, he said. It were either Petersburg or Moscow – I can't remember now.

Admittedly, Ferapont has never been to Moscow – 'It wasn't God's will' (*Ne privel Bog*, Act II). The sisters, too, rely on God, or fate, or chance, to determine the likelihood of their return to Moscow. In Act II Fedotik lays out the cards for a game of patience:

> IRINA. I can see, the game's going to come out. We shall get to Moscow.
> FEDOTIK. No, it's not going to come out. See, the eight's on top of the two of spades. (*He laughs.*) So you won't be getting to Moscow.

By Act IV Irina is resigned to 'fate' and to 'God's will' as far as Moscow is concerned:

> If I'm not destined to live in Moscow, then so be it. That's my fate. And there's nothing to be done about it... Everything is in the hands of God,[99] and that's the truth...

Olga also recognises in the final act: 'Nothing ever happens as we'd like it to. I didn't set out to be a headmistress, and yet now I am one. So Moscow

---

actually living there. Happiness is not for us...'.

98 Several commentators have detected a parallel between the literal burning of Moscow in 1812 and the metaphorical 'burning' or destruction of the sisters' dream of Moscow by Act III.

99 '*Vsë v Bozh'ei vole*' – more literally, 'Everything is God's will'.

is out of the question...'[100]

The play therefore ends, as it begins, with the journey to Moscow untaken. Another piece, written half a century later, comes to mind:

> VLADIMIR. Well? Shall we go?
> ESTRAGON. Yes, let's go.
> *They do not move.*
> CURTAIN[101]

It may be tempting for those accustomed to the semblance of meaningful activity to deride Olga, Masha, and Irina (and Vladimir and Estragon). 'Passivity' does not appeal to the 'practical' and hard-bitten, to people who pride themselves on being energetic and 'successful', self-assertive and 'illusion-free'.[102] Yet perhaps these 'inactive' characters appreciate that it is wiser not to play one's final card, and that to travel hopefully (or not travel at all) is better than to arrive.

In 1903 (mid-way between the play's first production and the unrest of 1905) the Communist and Marxist Anatoly Lunacharsky could feel no sympathy for the sisters' sorrowing languor:

> All the characters in *Three Sisters*, in our opinion, are worthy of derision, and the vulgar sister-in-law of the heroines is scarcely any more vulgar than the notorious three sisters themselves... The three sisters are young, beautiful, educated, with a pension from their father (a general), and with their own house...,[103] yet they moan and weep for a quite unfathomable reason. Would you believe it, they want to go to Moscow! Heavens above, go to Moscow then, who on earth is stopping you?...

Lunacharsky refused to add his tears to the weeping of 'these stupid three sisters' who 'could not regulate their lives'.[104]

---

100 In the first draft, however, Olga still clung to her dream of Moscow: 'I'll serve for a little while [as headmistress] and then probably go to Moscow...' (XIII, 306)

101 The end of Samuel Beckett's *Waiting for Godot* (1955; French version, *En attendant Godot*, 1952).

102 E. Kalmanovsky eloquently protests against the mistaken cult of 'will-power', 'practicality' and 'success' – Chekhov's characters are guided by 'conscience' rather than 'will-power' (in *Zvezda* 1 [1966], pp. 210-11).

103 As if a pension and a house equalled happiness! [G. McV.]

104 A. Lunacharsky, 'O khudozhnike voobshche i nekotorykh khudozhnikakh v

In contrast, many years later, Peggy Ashcroft felt 'enormously sympathetic' towards Irina and her sisters, regarding them all as 'frustrated by provincialism, by the society they lived in, by the fact that they were an impoverished family, and they *had* seen better days':[105]

> Certainly, they don't achieve. But that people don't succeed doesn't seem to me to make them monsters. They are impoverished, unhappy, longing – like most people.[106]

Their failure to go to Moscow does not make them into failures, any more than does the loss of their house. Ironically, the dramatist himself shared this yearning for Moscow, as he chafed in his provincial Yalta exile:

> I miss Moscow. It's boring without Muscovites, and without Moscow newspapers, and without the Moscow church bells which I love so much...
>
> (*To V.M. Sobolevsky*, 6 January 1899)

> The weather's completely summery. There's no news. I'm not writing anything. I'm just waiting for you to give me the signal to pack and to come to Moscow. Moscow...Moscow! These words are now the refrain not of *Three Sisters*, but of *One Husband...*
>
> (*To O.L. Knipper-Chekhova*, 21 November 1903)

Time – Past and Present

Discontented with their present life, the Prozorov children look to a golden past in Moscow, which they seek to translate into a golden future. If Natasha is the 'villainess' of the piece, then time may be regarded as the villain.

---

chastnosti', *Russkaia mysl'* 2 (Moscow, 1903), pp. 59, 60. In 1936 Osip Mandelstam maintained: 'There is no action in his dramas... If one handed out tickets – to the "three sisters", for instance – then the play would end' (*Sobranie sochinenii* IV [Paris, 1981], p. 108).

105 In Act I Masha regrets : 'In the old days, when Father was alive, we'd always have thirty or forty officers at our name-day parties, it was very lively, but today we get only a man and a half, and it's as silent as in the desert...'. In the play's opening speech Olga remarks that, a year ago, not many people came to their father's funeral.

106 Peggy Ashcroft's words, in 1987 and 1989, quoted in *Chekhov on the British Stage*, edited by Patrick Miles (1993), p. 89.

On one level, time plays a seemingly 'neutral' role in providing an outer framework for the action. The Queen's Theatre programme for Michel Saint-Denis' 1938 production drew attention to the season and time of day: 'Act I: Midday. Spring'; 'Act II: 8.15 p.m. Winter'; 'Act III: 2 a.m. Summer'; 'Act IV: Midday. Autumn'.

From the springtime of arrival in Act I to the autumn of farewells in Act IV, the characters are forever conscious of time and transience. This becomes apparent as soon as the curtain rises:

> OLGA. It's exactly a year since Father died – on this very day, the fifth of May – your name-day, Irina. It was snowing then, and very cold. I thought I'd never get over it, and you had fainted and were lying there, quite still, as if you were dead. But now a year's gone by, and we can talk about it calmly. You're wearing white again, and your face is radiant...
>
> *The clock strikes twelve.*
>
> The clock was striking then, too.
>
> *Pause.*

References to time pervade the entire play. Kulygin remarks (Act I) that the family clock is seven minutes fast – although the unfortunate pedant himself is noticeably slow (in Acts II, III, and IV) in catching up with his errant wife. Photographs (Acts I and IV) attempt to freeze time, while the nihilistic Chebutykin tries to confuse or even destroy time – the sixty-year-old doctor, whose own life has 'flashed past like lightning', claims he is 'thirty-two' (Act II), and he smashes (half-deliberately?) a porcelain or china clock in Act III.

Few other plays convey so keenly the ageing of the characters. When dramatic action is confined within twenty-four hours, the plot may appear dynamic and the protagonists busily purposeful. In *Three Sisters*, however, where time elapses inconspicuously and yet inexorably between the acts,[107] compression is replaced by prolonged frustration. 'We have time to grow old.'[108]

'How time flies! (*Kak idet vremia!*)' (Vershinin, Act I); 'Oh, how much older you look!' (Masha to Vershinin, Act I); 'But you haven't a single grey hair. You look older, but you're not old' (Olga to Vershinin, Act I); 'My hair is turning grey, I'm nearly an old man already' (Vershinin, Act II).[109]

---

107 As well as (more conspicuously) within each act.

108 Vladimir's words, in Act II of *Waiting for Godot*.

109 On 7 February 1903 Chekhov was to write to his wife, Olga

'I'm twenty years old!' (Irina, Act I); 'I'm already twenty-three...' (Irina, Act III).

'Oh youth, wonderful, beautiful youth!... My heart is full of love and joy... I love you, love you...as I have never loved anyone...' (Andrei to Natasha, end of Act I); 'I was just thinking... Anyway, there's nothing to say...' (Andrei to Natasha, start of Act II).

The flow of time seems to bring destruction rather than new creation; memories fade, without replenishment. The characters in *Three Sisters* are preoccupied with forgetting, and being forgotten.

'I remember there were three girls. I no longer remember your faces...' (Vershinin, Act I).

Masha says of her dead mother: 'I'm already beginning to forget her face. And we shan't be remembered, either. We shall be forgotten'. Vershinin replies: 'Yes. We shall be forgotten. Such is our fate...' (Act I).

Chebutykin does not remember the treatment for Andrei's shortness of breath (Act II), and in his Act III drunkenness he gloomily asserts: 'They think I'm a doctor and that I can cure all kinds of diseases, but I know absolutely nothing, I've forgotten everything I knew, I don't remember a thing, absolutely nothing...'.

When Tuzenbakh and Kulygin enthuse that Masha plays the piano 'splendidly' (Act III), Irina retorts: 'She's already forgotten how to. She hasn't played for three years...or four'.[110]

Perhaps the most poignant instance of forgetting stems from Irina later in that act, as she sobs:

> Where? Where has it all gone? Where is it? Oh my God! I've forgotten it all, forgotten... My head's in such a muddle... I can't remember the Italian for 'window' or 'ceiling'... I'm forgetting it all, every day I forget, and life is slipping away and will never come back, we shall never, never go to Moscow... I can see that we won't go...

Knipper-Chekhova: 'Time is passing quickly, very quickly! My beard has turned quite grey, and I have no desires at all...'.

110 The music-loving Chekhov was keenly aware of the poignancy of the piano image. In Act IV Irina declares: 'My soul is like an expensive piano, which is locked and the key is lost'. At the end of Act II of *Uncle Vanya*, the selfish Serebryakov prevents Elena from playing the piano. Chafing in his Yalta 'prison', Chekhov had himself written to his sister Masha on 11 November 1899: 'The piano and I are the two objects in this house which exist in silence, wondering why we were placed here when there is no one to play us...'.

In such moments of depression or despair – 'And time is passing...' (Irina, Act III) – one might explode:

> Have you not done tormenting me with your accursed time! It's abominable! When! When! One day, is that not enough for you, one day like any other day, one day he went dumb, one day I went blind, one day we'll go deaf, one day we were born, one day we shall die, the same day, the same second, is that not enough for you? (*Calmer.*) They give birth astride of a grave, the light gleams an instant, then it's night once more. (*He jerks the rope.*) On![111]

Or, more ruminatively, one may reflect:

> Time, like an ever-rolling stream,
> Bears all its sons away;
> They fly forgotten, as a dream
> Dies at the opening day...[112]

In her closing lines, Olga declares:

> Time will pass, and we shall depart for ever, people will forget us, forget our faces, voices, and how many of us there were...

Yet they are *not* forgotten. The three sisters and their friends have transcended time, and – without a trace of pretentiousness – have become symbols of undying aspiration.

Philosophising and the Future

If the passing of time is a cause for regret (linked with fading dreams and forgetfulness), then thoughts of the future may console (with the undashed hopes of time yet unspent). Caught in a triple time trap, with the unsatisfying present lying between the unrecoverable past and an undiscoverable future, Chekhov's characters readily speculate about what is yet to come.[113]

---

111 Pozzo's last words, in Act II of *Waiting for Godot*.

112 From the hymn by I. Watts (1674-1748), which begins with the consoling lines: 'O God, our help in ages past, / Our hope for years to come...'.

113 'Practical' wisdom might suggest that they should try to live more in the

The two figures most given to 'philosophising' about the future are Vershinin and Tuzenbakh. Their debates have a certain symmetry: one protagonist begins to talk, the other then joins in, and soon the initiator breaks off the discussion. Undoubtedly, there is something comic about these verbal duels – both men seem rather ineffectual individuals, who may be seeking (whether consciously or not) to impress susceptible females.[114] An unsympathetic listener might dismiss their perorations as idle prattle, repetitive, banal, and vacuous.

Yet, despite the comic overtones so typical of Chekhov, these 'philosophical' speeches extend the play's horizons, inducing in the characters on stage, as in the readers or audience, a mood of reflectiveness, inquiry, and expectation. It is significant that, at the Moscow Arts Theatre in the early years of this century, both Stanislavsky and Kachalov appeared highly sympathetic in the roles of Vershinin and Tuzenbakh, respectively.[115] A Soviet critic has wisely remarked: 'It is quite wrong to label Vershinin and Tuzenbakh as eccentrics: for Chekhov, dreaming is not eccentricity but the moral norm'.[116] V. Lakshin comments perceptively that, although 'their philosophy is naive, and their speeches at times are Utopian and starry-eyed', Vershinin and Tuzenbakh 'gain our sympathy through their spiritual unrest and their intellectual culture':

---

present, rather than in the past or future – yet to do so could mean settling for mediocrity rather than striving for the ideal. In a way, to be human means to be aware of the past and of the future, and not merely to exist in the present. In a notebook Chekhov observed: 'If you work for the sake of the present moment, your work will prove worthless; one must work, bearing only the future in mind. Mankind will live for the present moment, perhaps only in paradise; it [mankind] has always lived in the future' (XVII, 17).

114 Thus, as they talk, Vershinin may have Masha in mind, and Tuzenbakh – Irina.

115 One critic felt that the role of Vershinin was 'exceptionally dear' to both author and actor. Stanislavsky's Vershinin (which marked the 'peak [*vershina*] of psychological realism' on stage) was 'a tender, pure soul', 'radiant', yet also 'shy, bashful, smiling timidly' – see Nikolai Efros, *K.S. Stanislavskii (Opyt kharakteristiki)* (Petersburg, 1918), pp. 84, 86.

From the autumn of 1902 Vasily Kachalov acted the part of Tuzenbakh. According to Efros, Chekhov was 'absolutely delighted' by Kachalov's sympathetic portrait of the Baron, which combined quiet sorrow and affectionate humour. 'Both Chekhov and Kachalov love Tuzenbakh and gently make fun of him...' – see Nikolai Efros, *V.I. Kachalov (Fragment)* (Petersburg, 1919), pp. 49-50.

116 A. Roskin, 'Opasnosti i soblazny', *Teatr* 1 (Moscow, January 1960), p. 115. Harvey Pitcher writes: 'Vershinin is the successor to Astrov in *Uncle Vanya*. If Astrov's name suggests the stars, then that of Vershinin suggests *vershina*, meaning "peak" or "summit". Like Astrov Vershinin appears to be concerned not so much with his own personal life as with life in general...' (*The Chekhov Play: A New Interpretation* [London, 1973], p. 144).

> The characters' thoughts about work, the future, and man's vocation raise them above ordinary life (*byt*), above the trivia of everyday, and cast a ray of hope upon the cheerlessness of philistine life.
>
> The entire charm of Chekhov's plays lies in this lyrical and intellectual atmosphere...[117]

'Philosophical' or 'intellectual' moments occur in every act of the play. In Act I, Masha's comment about the past (her dead mother) prompts Vershinin to meditate upon the future:

> MASHA. Can you imagine, I'm already beginning to forget her face. And we shan't be remembered, either. We shall be forgotten.
>
> VERSHININ. Yes. We shall be forgotten. Such is our fate, and there's nothing we can do about it. The things that seem so serious, significant, and highly important to us now will in time be forgotten or seem quite unimportant.
>
> *Pause.*
>
> And it's interesting to note that we can't possibly know now what eventually will be thought elevated and important, and what will be considered trivial and absurd. Didn't the discoveries made by Copernicus – or Columbus, for example – appear useless and absurd at first, whereas some empty nonsense (*vzdor*) written by a crank seemed like a revelation? And it may well be that our present life, which we accept so meekly, will in time seem strange, uncomfortable, foolish, not as pure as it should be – perhaps even sinful...
>
> TUZENBAKH. Who knows? Perhaps our life will be thought elevated and remembered with respect. There's no torture now, no executions or invasions, and yet at the same time there is so much suffering!
>
> SOLYONY (*in a high-pitched voice*). Cheep, cheep, cheep... If there's one thing the Baron loves it's a nice bit of philosophising.

---

117 V. Lakshin, *Tolstoi i Chekhov* (Moscow, 1963), pp. 261-2. Another critic notes: 'Vershinin and Tuzenbakh argue heatedly about the better future, but we pay no attention to the difference in their views and we soon forget where this difference lies; the important thing is that they are both longing for a better future, just as the sisters long for Moscow' (B. Zingerman, *Teatr Chekhova i ego mirovoe znachenie* [Moscow, 1988], pp. 360-1).

TUZENBAKH. Vasily Vasilyich, will you please leave me alone... (*Sits elsewhere.*) It's becoming rather tiresome.
SOLYONY (*in a high-pitched voice*). Cheep, cheep, cheep...
TUZENBAKH (*to Vershinin*). The suffering we now observe – and there's so much of it about! – does nevertheless testify to a certain moral upsurge evident in society...
VERSHININ. Yes, yes, of course.

At this point the 'debate' breaks down, following an intervention by Chebutykin and the sound of Andrei's violin-playing off-stage – but Vershinin's weak 'Yes, yes, of course' suggests that the Lieutenant-Colonel wishes to rest his tongue for a while. He resumes, however, after a few minutes, when he responds to Masha's defeatism by offering an optimistic vision of the future:

ANDREI. Thanks to Father, my sisters and I know French, German and English, while Irina knows Italian as well. But what it cost us!
MASHA. Knowing three languages in a town like this is a superfluous luxury. Not even a luxury, but a kind of superfluous appendage, like a sixth finger. We know a great deal that's useless.
VERSHININ. Do you really? (*He laughs.*) You know a great deal that's useless! In my opinion, there isn't a town on earth which is so dull and dreary as to render an intelligent and educated person 'superfluous'. Let's suppose that in this town – which, indeed, is coarse and backward – there are only three people like you in a population of a hundred thousand. Obviously, you won't prevail over the mass of darkness around you; in the course of your life you'll gradually have to give way and become lost in that crowd of a hundred thousand, life will choke you, and yet you won't disappear, you shan't remain without influence; after you, perhaps there'll be six people like you, then twelve and so on, until eventually people like you form the majority.[118] In two or three hundred years' time life on earth will be unimaginably beautiful and marvellous. Man needs a life like that,

118 Later, in Act III, Vershinin envisages the time when 'more and more' people will live as the three sisters now do, 'and then you too [that is, the three sisters] will become out of date, and people will be born who are better than you...'.

> and if as yet it doesn't exist, then he must eagerly anticipate it, wait, dream and prepare for it, and this means he has to see and know more than his grandfather and father before him. (*He laughs.*) And you complain that you know a great deal that's 'useless'.
>
> MASHA (*taking off her hat*). I'm staying for lunch.
>
> IRINA (*with a sigh*). Goodness, someone should have written all that down...
>
> *Andrei has walked off-stage, unnoticed.*
>
> TUZENBAKH. You say that, many years from now, life on earth will be beautiful and marvellous. I agree. But, in order to share in it now, if only from afar, we must prepare for it, we must work...
>
> VERSHININ (*standing up*). Yes. But what a lot of flowers you've got!...

A few moments later, Vershinin reflects:

> I often think: supposing we could start our life afresh, but fully conscious this time? If the one life we've already lived could be a rough draft, as it were, whereas the second chance would be the fair copy! In that case each one of us, I think, would try above all not to repeat himself, or at least he'd create different conditions for his life, he'd choose for himself accommodation like this, with flowers and a blaze of light...[119] I have a wife and two little girls, what's more my wife is in poor health and so on and so forth, but if I could start my life again, I wouldn't get married... No, no!

The forlorn desire to 'start one's life afresh' may seem rather clichéd and banal (and Vershinin's predictable mention of his 'wife and two little girls' provokes a smile) – and yet this is a thought expressed by many of Chekhov's characters, and one which strikes a basic chord in the reader's or audience's heart.

In Act II, while deprived of a cup of tea, Vershinin and Tuzenbakh speculate once more about life in 'two or three hundred years' time', and

---

119 'Blaze of light' – Vershinin unconsciously uses the same two words (*massa sveta*) spoken by Olga earlier in the act ('I woke up this morning, and saw a blaze of light...'). The phrase forms a direct contrast to the '*temnaia massa*' ('mass of darkness') of the surrounding population.

about the possibility (or impossibility) of happiness. This series of reflections forms one of the most meditative and 'atmospheric' sections of the entire play.[120]

The Act III fire then leads Vershinin to further contemplation about his two young daughters: 'My God, I thought, what more will these girls have to endure in the course of a long life!'[121] He continues:

> And when my little girls were standing on the doorstep in their nightclothes, barefooted, and the street was red from the flames, and the noise was terrifying, it struck me that something very similar used to happen many years ago, when the enemy suddenly attacked, plundering and burning... And yet, in actual fact, what a difference there is between then and now! And in a little while, in some two or three hundred years, people will regard our present life too with horror and derision; everything about our present times will appear awkward, and oppressive, and extremely inconvenient, and strange. Oh, what a life it's going to be, surely, what a life! (*He laughs.*) Forgive me, I'm off philosophising again. Please allow me to continue, ladies and gentlemen. I feel a great urge to philosophise, I'm in the mood right now.
>
> *Pause.*
>
> They all seem to be asleep...

And so the enamoured Vershinin philosophises on, heard only by his beloved Masha, with whom he soon exchanges their love-call ('Tram-tam-tam...').

In Act IV, while awaiting his final farewell with Masha, Vershinin again passes the time in speculation:

> OLGA (*wiping her eyes*). Why isn't Masha coming?...
> VERSHININ. What else can I say as I bid you farewell? What little piece of philosophising?... (*He laughs.*) Life is hard. To many of us it appears blank and hopeless, and yet one has to admit that it's gradually becoming easier and brighter, and it seems the time is not far off when life will be quite radiant. (*He looks at his watch.*) I really must be going! In the old days the human race

120 Already quoted in the section on 'Happiness' (pp. 39-42 above).
121 With hindsight, one can answer: war, revolution, Stalin, terror.

was occupied by wars, filling its entire existence with campaigns and raids and conquests. But now that's all a thing of the past, and it has left a huge vacuum which as yet cannot be filled. Mankind is seeking passionately, and will, of course, find.[122] Oh, if only it could happen soon!

Pause.

You know, if education could be allied with diligence, and diligence with education. (*He looks at his watch.*) But I really must go...

OLGA. Here she is.

Enter Masha.

VERSHININ. I've come to say goodbye...

Olga steps slightly to one side, so as not to hinder their leave-taking.

MASHA (*gazing at his face*). Goodbye...

A prolonged kiss.

As Chekhov's characters long for personal happiness, so they yearn for the future happiness of mankind. In Act IV, after lamenting his vanished past, Andrei exclaims: 'The present is hateful, but when I think of the future, how good it feels!...'.

Chekhov himself, although openly critical of 'our inert, apathetic, lazily philosophising,[123] cold intellectuals' (letter of 27 December 1889), was less willing to pontificate concerning the past, present, and future. In certain letters, however, he did express a reluctance to idealise the past (or present), and his confidence in a better future:

> I have no faith in our intelligentsia, which is hypocritical, false, hysterical, ill-bred, lazy. I have no faith in it even when it suffers and complains, for its oppressors come from its own midst. I believe in individual people, I see salvation in individuals scattered the length and breadth of Russia – be they intellectuals or peasants – for they possess strength, even though they are few in number...
>
> (*To I.I. Orlov*, 22 February 1899)

---

122 Cf. 'Seek, and ye shall find' (Matthew 7:7).

123 Chekhov uses here the same verb as in *Three Sisters* for 'to philosophise' (*filosofstvovat'*): '*Vialaia, apatichnaia, lenivo filosofstvuiushchaia, kholodnaia intelligentsiia...*'. It seems highly doubtful that, eleven years later, he would have wished to consign Vershinin and Tuzenbakh to such a negative category, merely on the basis of a shared propensity for 'philosophising'.

> All I can see and, fortunately, understand is that life and people are becoming better and better, more intelligent and honest – that's in important matters, whereas smaller matters have already merged in my eyes into a monochrome grey field, for I no longer see as I used to...
>
> (*To V.L. Kign*, 10 November 1903)

Religion and Meaning

Three Sisters is not a play about religion, although it has been regarded by some critics as an intrinsically religious play. It contains one remarkably heartfelt affirmation (by Masha, in Act II):

> It seems to me that man must have faith or seek faith, for otherwise his life is empty, empty... How can you live and not know why the cranes fly, why children are born, why there are stars in the sky... Either you know why you live, or everything's pointless, mere straw in the wind.[124]

Chekhov's more sensitive characters are acutely aware of the fragility of life, and their defencelessness before the ever-rolling stream of Time. In his letter to Suvorin on 27 October 1888 Chekhov had explained: 'An artist observes, selects, conjectures, arranges – and these very acts presuppose as their starting-point a question – for if from the start he's not set himself a question, there would be nothing to conjecture or select...'. In Chekhov's statement the words 'An artist' could be replaced not merely by 'A critic', but also by 'A Chekhovian character'. When Vershinin and Tuzenbakh choose to 'philosophise' about happiness or the future of mankind, and Masha indicates the importance of faith, 'these very acts presuppose as their starting-point a question'. The basic question is: why do we live, and what is the meaning of our suffering?

A pessimistic answer is offered by the Preacher of Ecclesiastes:

---

124 These words (as with Tuzenbakh's Act I prophecy of the imminent 'storm') are often singled out by critics for discussion. On a separate sheet Chekhov offered variations of Masha's thought: 'Man will continue to go astray, seek a purpose, and be dissatisfied, until he discovers his God. It is impossible to live [merely] for the sake of one's children or mankind. And if there is no God, then there is no point in living, one must perish' (XVII, 215-6); 'Man must either have faith or seek faith, for otherwise he is an empty person' (XVII, 216).

> Vanity of vanities, saith the Preacher, vanity of vanities; all is vanity.
> What profit hath a man of all his labour which he taketh under the sun?...
> All go unto one place; all are of the dust, and all turn to dust again...[125]

In his Act III intoxication, Chebutykin questions the reality of 'existence' and longs for non-existence:

> I did know something twenty-five years or so ago, but now I can't remember anything. Not a thing... In my head there is emptiness, in my soul it is cold. Perhaps I'm not even a human being, and I just go about pretending that I've got arms and legs...and a head; perhaps I don't even exist at all, and I'm just imagining that I walk, and eat, and sleep. (*He weeps.*) Oh, if only I could be non-existent!...

Shortly afterwards, he drops and breaks a clock, which Irina says belonged to her dead mother. Chebutykin morosely retorts:

> Perhaps it did... If it was your mother's, then it was your mother's. Perhaps I didn't break it – and it only seems I did. Perhaps it only seems to us that we exist, but in fact we aren't here at all. I don't know anything, nobody knows anything...

Throughout the fourth act, Chebutykin presents a front of indifference (to shield himself from the pain of existence?). His watchword becomes '*Vsë ravno!*' ('It's all the same!', 'It doesn't matter!', 'Nothing matters!', 'Who cares?', 'What difference does it make?').[126]

If Chebutykin's voice is given prominence – and Tuzenbakh's Act II remark, 'Meaning?... It's snowing outside. What's the meaning of that?' – one conclusion might be reached: 'Indifference is the mode of the play, not

---

125 Ecclesiastes 1:2-3, 3:20. Various critics have linked Chekhov's outlook with that of Ecclesiastes. See also XVII, 194, 438-9.

126 Commentators have noted how frequently the phrase *vsë ravno* is spoken in *Three Sisters*. When revising the play, Chekhov intensified its recurrence as a linguistic leitmotif for the nihilistic Chebutykin. *Vsë ravno* is uttered by many other characters (including Masha, Andrei, Kulygin, Tuzenbakh, Solyony, and Natasha) with a variety of intonation. Besides indifference, the phrase may convey defiance and a devil-may-care attitude.

optimism; indifference to a world that offers only indifference in return'.[127] Recurrent references to God might be interpreted as revealing a fateful passivity in various characters – 'God willing, it will all turn out as we hope' (Irina, Act I); 'All is well, everything comes from God'[128] (Olga, Act I); 'It wasn't God's will' (Ferapont, Act II); 'But if it were God's will that he should marry you, then I'd be happy' (Olga to Irina, concerning Tuzenbakh, Act III); 'Somehow God will help me!' (Irina, Act IV).[129] 'Everything is in the hands of God' (Irina, Act IV). Yet it would seem more accurate to suggest that *yearning* is the true 'mode' of the play, not indifference or optimism, and that the reliance on God's will is not passivity, but rather, a humble recognition of human ignorance and powerlessness.

Chekhov may have aspired to 'objectivity' in his writing, allowing his readers the role of 'jury'. Nothing could be simpler than to emphasise the three sisters' manifest shortcomings – Irina's naivety and dreaminess, Masha's moodiness and occasional coarseness, Olga's ineffectiveness and 'old-maidishness'. Yet it should be equally manifest that such shortcomings do not constitute mortal sins, and that the longings of the sisters and their friends lend an essentially religious (or spiritual, or moral) dimension to the entire play.

Certain leitmotifs in Chekhov's plays and short stories, and the evidence of his own life, suggest that the Prozorov family and their friends avoid most of the negative characteristics from which Chekhov recoiled. They are *not* petty, boorish, cruel, drunken, dirty, crude, philistine, empty, self-satisfied, blinkered and hypocritical. They do not reduce the purpose of life to growing gooseberries (*Gooseberries*), enforcing prohibitions and restrictions (*Sergeant Prishibeev* [*Unter Prishibeev*], 1885, and *The Man in a Case*), accumulating money (*Ionych*, 1898), or pursuing celebrity, status, and casual 'love' affairs (*The Grasshopper* [*Poprygun'ia*], 1891). They are kindly, aspiring, forgivably foolish, vulnerable, and completely human. Whereas Natasha is unutterably vulgar, and aesthetically and morally barbarous, the three sisters and their closest friends (above all, Vershinin, Tuzenbakh, Andrei,

---

127 Michael Frayn, in the introduction to his translation of *Three Sisters* (London and New York, 1983), p. xiii.

128 '*Vsë khorosho, vsë ot Boga*'. Chekhov himself used the last three words in a letter of 18 November 1891.

129 Anfisa in Act IV is overjoyed that 'the Lord' (*Gospod'*) has provided a room for her old age. The word *Bog* (God) occurs also in Act IV in idiomatic expressions of goodwill, when bidding farewell – '*Letite s Bogom!*' (Chebutykin to the birds, literally, 'Fly with God!'); '*Ukhodite s Bogom*' (Anfisa to the musicians, literally, 'Go with God').

and, to a certain extent, Chebutykin)[130] strive for spiritual, non-materialistic goals and long for a life that is happier, more beautiful, and more meaningful.

One critic has perceptively noted that 'Chekhov's characters can best be understood...by imagining them arranged on a continuum that stretches from the lackey to the free man, from the barbarian to the person of genuine culture, from spiritual deadness to sensitivity to life'.[131] Judged by these criteria, it would seem that the three sisters are 'free' spirits, embodying 'genuine culture' and 'sensitivity to life', whereas Natasha is a 'lackey' and 'barbarian', steeped in 'spiritual deadness'.[132]

The three sisters inhabit a different spiritual universe from their grubbily earth-bound sister-in-law. Throughout the play, Natasha relentlessly serves 'mammon'.[133] Natasha represents the body, with 'well-scrubbed cheeks' (Masha's description of her in Act I), unconvincingly denying her surfeit of flesh (in front of the mirror in Act III).[134] Her bodily 'raiment' reflects her being – 'a weird kind of skirt in a shade of bright yellow, with such a vulgar little fringe, and a red blouse' (Masha's words in Act I), 'a pink dress with a green belt' (stage direction in Act I), a dressing-gown (start of Act II), followed by a fur coat and cap (end of Act II). As the action unfolds, Natasha is revealed as 'a petty, blind, rough-skinned animal. At all events she's not a human being...' (Andrei's description of his wife in Act IV). Hence, her 'victory' in Act IV (in usurping the house) is entirely hollow:

> For what shall it profit a man, if he shall gain the whole world, and lose his own soul?[135]

---

130 That is, Chebutykin in his good-natured, grieving, lonely, and conscience-stricken aspects, but not in his drunken, cynical nihilism.

131 Kenneth A. Lantz, in *A Chekhov Companion*, edited by Toby W. Clyman (Westport, Connecticut, and London, 1985), p. 84.

132 E. Broide even suggests: 'The Natashas of this world are the future Chiefs [or Bosses] of concentration camps' (*Chekhov: Myslitel'. Khudozhnik* [Frankfurt/Main, 1980], p. 93).

133 See Matthew 6:24-25.

134 Concerning Natasha's stoutness in Act III, Stanislavsky surmised in his production score (p. 199): 'I'll tell you a secret: she's in the family way (literally, she's in an interesting condition [*ona v interesnom polozhenii*])'. There seems, however, to be no other hint in Acts III or IV to confirm Stanislavsky's hypothesis.

135 Mark 8:36; see also Matthew 16:26. It is not, of course, Natasha's stoutness, or even her physicality, which is intrinsically at fault – it is her lack of sensitivity and spirituality.

Indeed, unlike most of the other characters, Natasha gives no evidence of having a soul (*dusha*).[136] This is not to suggest that she is literally 'diabolical' or 'demonic'.[137] In a way, she is worse than that. In her affected embarrassment, her pretensions to pseudo-culture (the clashing clothes and mangled French), her cloying diminutives[138] and brusque commands, her military orderliness (rearranging the Prozorovs to suit her offspring, sweeping up redundant candles [Act II], aged servants [Act III], and forks [Act IV]), and in her total failure to appreciate the true beauty of children, and old people, and trees, and music, and love, Natasha is the very embodiment of *poshlost'*, all the more horrifying because of her veneer of gentility and reasonableness.

In the closing moments of the play, while Natasha continues to bluster and rage, the dispossessed sisters stay in the garden, their thoughts still fixed on other realms:

> *The three sisters stand huddled together.*
> MASHA. Oh, listen to the band! They're leaving us, one has gone for ever, never to return,[139] and we shall remain alone,

---

136 The word *dusha*, whose basic meaning is 'soul', may at times be translated as 'heart'. The numerous references to *dusha* (as to *Bog*, God) cause difficulties for English translators, and yet they form part of the 'spiritual' atmosphere of the play. *Three Sisters* abounds in such statements as: 'my heart is full of love and joy' (*dusha polna liubvi, vostorga*, Andrei, Act I); 'my soul [or my heart] is like an expensive piano' (*dusha moia kak dorogoi roial'*, Irina, Act IV). Recalling his dead patient in Act III, Chebutykin declares that 'in my soul it is cold' (*na dushe kholodno*); he feels that his soul is 'twisted, vile, disgusting' (*stalo na dushe krivo, gadko, merzko*). Before making her Act III 'confession', Masha says: 'My soul is languishing' (or 'My heart is pining', *Tomitsia dusha moia*). Natasha never utters the word *dusha*. Virginia Woolf commented on Chekhov's works in general: 'In reading Tchekov we find ourselves repeating the word "soul" again and again. It sprinkles his pages...' ('The Russian Point of View', in her *The Common Reader* [London, 1942; first published 1925], p. 225).

137 David Magarshack, however, emphasises Natasha's 'fascinatingly Satanic character', 'Natasha's truly devilish character' (*The Real Chekhov* [London, 1972], pp. 140, 181).

138 For example, she addresses her husband (Andrei) as 'Andryusha' and even 'Andryushanchik' (Act II); Bobik supposedly looks at her 'with his dear little eyes', 'with his eyesy-piesies' (*svoimi glazenochkami*, Act II); she will promenade with Protopopov 'for a teensy quarter of an hour' (*na chetvert' chasika*, Act II); when she has chopped down the fir-trees, she will replace them by masses of 'sweet little flowers' (*tsvetochkov, tsvetochkov*, she enthusiastically intones, Act IV).

139 That is, Tuzenbakh, whose death has been reported by Chebutykin. Off-stage,

to start our life again. We must go on living... We must go on living...[140]

IRINA (*rests her head on Olga's breast*). The time will come when people will understand everything, why these things happen, what the purpose is of all this suffering, there will be no more mysteries. But meanwhile we must go on living...we must go on working, just working! Tomorrow I'll leave alone, I shall teach at the school and devote my entire life to those who may need it. It's autumn now, winter will soon be here, covering everything with snow, but I shall work, I shall work...

OLGA (*embraces both her sisters*). The band is playing so cheerfully and jauntily – you really feel you want to live! Merciful God! Time will pass, and we shall depart for ever, people will forget us, forget our faces, voices, and how many of us there were, but our sufferings will turn to joy for those who live after us, happiness and peace will reign upon earth, and people will remember with a kind word and bless[141] those who are living now. My dear sisters, our life is not ended yet. We shall live! The band is playing so cheerfully, so joyously, and it seems that, in a little while, we shall know why we live, why we suffer... If only we knew, if only we knew!

The music grows fainter and fainter; Kulygin, cheerful and smiling, brings Masha's hat and cloak; Andrei pushes the other perambulator with Bobik sitting in it.

CHEBUTYKIN (*singing quietly*). Ta-ra-ra-boom-de-ay... I'm sitting down today...[142] (*Reads his newspaper.*) It doesn't

---

the soldiers are departing (evidently for Poland), to the sound of a military band.

140 In an earlier manuscript, Chekhov at this point gave Masha some further words (which were then regrettably omitted as Olga Knipper found them difficult to say): '(*She looks up at the sky*). Above us are the migrating birds, they have been flying, every spring and autumn, for thousands of years, and they don't know why, yet they fly and will go on flying for a long, long time to come, for many thousands of years – until at last God reveals to them his mysteries...' (XIII, 308, 433).

141 Olga uses here the verb *blagosloviat* (bless), just as the preceding speech by Irina contains the words 'there will be no more mysteries' (*nikakikh ne budet tain*). Some translators needlessly secularise Chekhov's vocabulary at such points.

142 'Ta-ra-ra-boom-de-ay' is the title of a song (1891) by Henry J. Sayers. Chekhov's rhyming Russian text literally says: 'I'm sitting on a kerbstone [or bollard]...' ('*Tara...ra...bumbiia...sizhu na tumbe ia...*'). The following lines,

matter! It doesn't matter!
OLGA. If only we knew, if only we knew![143]
Curtain.

The play thus ends with the journey incomplete, and the great questions unanswered ('why we live, why we suffer'). The awareness of sorrow, and of the 'vanity of vanities' of Ecclesiastes, is balanced, and perhaps even outweighed, by the yearning for peace, joy, and understanding.[144]

The three sisters and their friends are not models of perfection, nor are they always wise. A greater wisdom, perhaps, would be to accept life's frustrations and disappointments with equanimity, to learn to endure and to 'bear one's cross' without complaint. Something of this attitude is hinted at in the closing moments of *Three Sisters*, and in the distraught Nina's final speeches in Act IV of *The Seagull*, and in Sonya's last consoling words to Vanya in *Uncle Vanya*. The experience of these plays seems to suggest that one should not expect, or even seek, personal happiness – it is enough to persevere.[145]

Perhaps what Chekhov's sympathetic characters lack most is the confidence and consolation of a religious faith, or a linking 'general idea'. This theme recurs throughout Chekhov's writing, whenever characters painfully yearn for immortality, 'God', truth, beauty, or meaning, and usually grieve at the non-achievement of their goal.[146]

Chekhov steadfastly refuses to preach and solve. Nevertheless, for all

---

not quoted by Chekhov, are: 'And I weep bitterly/Because I'm so insignificant' (XIII, 466).

143 Olga's closing words, a fourfold *'Esli by znat'!'*, are extremely difficult to translate. 'If only we knew!' seems the neatest and most frequent rendition, although other versions include 'If we only knew!', 'If only we could know!'. Olga's aspiration contrasts with Chebutykin's nihilistic Act III wish: *'O, esli by ne sushchestvovat'!'* ('Oh, if only I could be non-existent!').

144 Cf. 'For now we see through a glass darkly; but then face to face: now I know in part; but then shall I know even as also I am known' (The First Epistle of Paul to the Corinthians 13:12).

145 Vsevolod Meyerhold (the first Tuzenbakh) wrote to Chekhov in December 1901: 'Thanks to you it is easier to live, because you inspire us with faith in a better future and you make us persevere [or endure (*terpet'*)]...' (quoted in V.E. Meyerhold, *Perepiska: 1896-1939* [Moscow, 1976], p. 34).

146 See, for instance, passages in *A Dreary Story (Skuchnaia istoriia)* (1889), *The Duel (Duel')* (1891), *Ward Number Six (Palata No. 6)* (1892), *The Student (Student)* (1894), *The House with the Mezzanine (Dom s mezoninom)* (1896), *Ionych*, *The Lady with the Dog (Dama s sobachkoi)* (1899), *The Bride (Nevesta)* (1903), and many other stories.

their human frailty, it seems not inappropriate to consider the Prozorov family and their friends in the words of the Beatitudes:

> Blessed are the poor in spirit: for theirs is the kingdom of heaven.
> Blessed are they that mourn: for they shall be comforted.
> Blessed are the meek: for they shall inherit the earth.
> Blessed are they which do hunger and thirst after righteousness: for they shall be filled.
> Blessed are the merciful: for they shall obtain mercy.
> Blessed are the pure in heart: for they shall see God...[147]

The question of 'Chekhov and religion' is a highly complex one. It is clear that, throughout his adult life, Chekhov was not a practising Orthodox believer, and his letters contain several declarations of disbelief: 'I have no religion now' (9 March 1892); 'I'm a non-believer' (28 January 1900); 'I lost my faith long ago' (12 July 1903). The scientific doctor who prized civilisation and economic progress rejected any form of hypocrisy, hysteria, obscurantism, or fashionable religiosity.

Yet Chekhov's temperament was far removed from that of the militant atheist. As his letters abundantly attest, he liked hearing church bells, visiting monasteries, and bestowing religious blessings on his correspondents. He could picture himself as a kind of secular monk, and advocate a solitary search for faith, 'all alone with one's conscience' (17 December 1901).[148]

Despite his habitual scepticism, Chekhov seems in many respects to have been a frustrated idealist, a would-be believer.[149] While lacking

---

147 Matthew 5:3-8. A similar view was expressed in 1910 by Kornei Chukovsky who perceived 'Christ' in the play, and a cry of 'hosanna to the meek and the poor in spirit'. Although the sisters' house may seem under a spell or curse, it is in fact a 'holy place' (*sviatynia*), and the sisters themselves are 'holy' (*sviaty*). Natasha and Protopopov 'commit sacrilege' (*sviatotatstvuiut*) near the sisters, 'but their sacrilege is powerless' (*Mir* 5 [1910], pp. 356-9).

148 Chekhov's notebooks provide further reflections on faith: 'Faith is a spiritual faculty. It is lacking in animals, while savages and undeveloped people have fear and doubts. Faith is accessible only to higher organisms' (XVII, 67).

149 Ivan Bunin recalls that Chekhov would often dismiss belief in immortality and life after death as 'nonsense', but would then assert the opposite even more forcefully, that 'immortality is a fact' and 'we shall definitely have life after death' (in *Chekhov v vospominaniiakh sovremennikov*, edited by A.K. Kotov [Moscow, 1954], p. 494). See also I.A. Bunin, *O Chekhove* (New York, 1955), pp. 98-9.

a metaphysical faith, he did not deride the sincere belief of others. It would seem fair to claim that his life, personality and works[150] are not incompatible with the spirit of Christianity, or with the loftiest form of humanism.

The religious or quasi-religious element in Chekhov should not be exaggerated, but nor should it be overlooked. It has been commented upon by various critics.[151] His letters frequently touch upon matters of religion and faith:

> Merezhk[ovsky] calls my monk, the one who composed hymns of praise to God,[152] a failure in his personal life. How is he a failure? God grant everyone a life like his: he believed in God, he had enough to eat, and he possessed creative talent...
>
> (*To A.S. Suvorin*, 3 November 1888)

> One ought to believe in God, but, if faith is absent, one shouldn't replace it by idle sensationalism, but instead seek and seek, seek all by oneself, all alone with one's conscience...
>
> (*To V.S. Mirolyubov*, 17 December 1901)

> One may say concerning the educated part of our society that it has moved away from religion and is moving further and further away from it, whatever people may say and no matter what kind of philosophical-religious societies may assemble. Whether that's good or bad I won't presume to judge, but I will say that the religious movement of which you write is one thing, and the whole of contemporary culture is another, and one shouldn't place the latter in causal dependence on the former. Present-day culture is the beginning of work in the name of a great future, work which will continue, perhaps, for tens of thousands of years so that, if only in the

---

150 See, for instance, his treatment of the religious theme in such stories as *Easter Eve* (*Sviatoiu noch'iu*) (1886), *The Student*, and *The Bishop* (*Arkhierei*) (1902).

151 In 1923 John Middleton Murry declared, albeit nebulously: 'Thomas Hardy and Anton Tchehov are the two truly religious writers of our time... There is no falseness in their souls or in their writings, but only purity... In the very manner of *their* asking: Does God exist? God is manifest...' (in *The Adelphi* 1, 3 [August 1923], pp. 181-2). See also W.H. Bruford, *Chekhov and his Russia: A Sociological Study* (London, 1947), pp. 128-9, 206, 209-10.

152 The monk Nikolai, in *Easter Eve*.

> distant future, mankind may perceive the truth of the real God – that is, not make conjectures or search for Him in Dostoevsky, but perceive clearly, just as it has perceived that twice two is four. Present-day culture is the beginning of this work, whereas the religious movement of which we spoke is a survival from the past, almost the end of what is now obsolete or obsolescent. Still, it's a long story, it can't all be put in a letter...
>
> (*To S.P. Diaghilev*, 30 December 1902)

Comedy

The emphasis, until this point, on such topics as love, work, happiness, time, religion and meaning may make *Three Sisters* sound like a dauntingly lugubrious piece. This is not, however, the case, for humour and comedy pervade the entire play. Vladimir Nemirovich-Danchenko, co-director of the first Moscow Arts Theatre production, even claims that Chekhov insisted that he had written a 'vaudeville', although the Arts Theatre company found his definition incomprehensible, 'since even in the manuscript *Three Sisters* was called a drama'.[153]

Of course, *Three Sisters* is not a 'vaudeville' in the light-hearted, almost farcical style of earlier works such as *The Bear* and *The Proposal* (1888). Nor are its characters, for the most part, as patently eccentric as many of the figures in *The Cherry Orchard*, which the dramatist himself designated as a 'comedy'. Yet it should be remembered that Chekhov began his literary career as a humorist, often under the pseudonym Antosha Chekhonte, and established his reputation in his native land as a purveyor of carefree bagatelles.

Three Sisters is a profoundly serious piece in the questions it raises, and the evolving themes of frustration and disillusionment are marked with sorrow. Many of the characters are intensely likeable. Yet hardly any theme or character in the play remains untouched by laughter. If, indeed, human beings are 'comic for forty-eight weeks in the year' (as Chekhov claimed in a letter of about March 1886), then it follows that nobody should take himself or herself over-earnestly.[154] In his 'Producer's Note' of 1967, Laurence Olivier referred to the 'slavish discipleship' which Chekhov 'evokes in his interpretative craftsmen':

---

153 Vl.Iv. Nemirovich-Danchenko, *Iz proshlogo* (Moscow, 1936), p. 217.

154 The humourless characters are the most comic, such as Professor Serebryakov in *Uncle Vanya*. In part, comedy is one aspect of Chekhov's sense of balance, perspective and detachment.

> Once his intentions are perceived, he is subject to (and indeed he would seem to delight in) a wide variety of interpretations, always excepting the ponderous. We remember how he insists that all his works be regarded as comedies... One may detect a slight note of self-deprecation in this, but one must take the hint boldly enough to ensure that what is serious must filter through a delicate lens composed of a tender awareness of human frailties and absurdities... To Chekhov the least desirable of human attitudes is the Earnest...[155]

If to be self-repeating is comic, then several characters have a comic predictability. After a short while, the reader or audience comes to expect Vershinin's philosophising about the future (and complaints about his wife), Solyony's Lermontov pose and perfumed hands,[156] Tuzenbakh's denial of his Germanic origins (though no one is accusing him of anything), Kulygin's Latin pedantry and veneration of his headmaster,[157] and Natasha's mangled French. Repeatedly, Andrei confides in the deaf Ferapont, Tuzenbakh jousts with Vershinin, Kulygin pursues his absent wife, Masha snaps and snarls, Natasha prowls and disrupts.

Solyony provides a strand of dark humour throughout the play. Constantly spoiling for a fight, he becomes involved in ludicrous arguments in Act II, as to whether Moscow has one or two universities, and over the definition of *chekhartma* and *cheremsha*.[158] Solyony offers unhelpful

---

155 Laurence Olivier, in the programme for *Three Sisters* at the National Theatre, London, 1967.

156 Solyony is forever sprinkling perfume on his hands (and, in Act I, on his chest), in a gesture which seems to combine affectation with a mounting awareness of his 'foul-smelling', murderous intent. After sprinkling his hands in Act IV, he states explicitly: 'I've used up a whole bottle today, and still they [his hands]...smell like a corpse.' In this respect (like Natasha with her candle in Act III) he may be regarded as a debased Lady Macbeth figure – in Act V of *Macbeth*, the sleepwalking Lady Macbeth obsessively rubs her hands and remarks: 'What, will these hands ne'er be clean?' In Act III of *Three Sisters*, Chebutykin also washes his hands, as if seeking to cleanse himself of his patient's death. In Lermontov's *A Hero of Our Time* (*Geroi nashego vremeni*) (1840) Grushnitsky liberally sprinkles himself with perfume.

157 By Act IV Kulygin has even become clean-shaven, in emulation of his superior.

158 Here Chebutykin and Solyony talk completely at cross purposes. Chebutykin claims that *chekhartma* is a Caucasian meat-dish (roast mutton), to which Solyony retorts that *cheremsha* is a kind of onion (with a garlic-like smell). The altercation becomes quite heated, although both men are perfectly correct

comments about the location of the railway station ('If the station were near, then it wouldn't be far, but if it's far, then it can't be near', Act I), and provides a couple of splendid conversation-stoppers – 'If that child were mine, I'd fry him in a frying-pan and eat him' (Act II, to Natasha), and (in Act I):

VERSHININ. The liqueur's delicious. What's it made of?
SOLYONY. Black beetles.[159]

In *Three Sisters*, there is much good humour between characters who know one another well and who revel in mutual teasing. In the first half of the play, a festive mood is fostered by particular seasonal events (Irina's name-day party in Act I, the awaited arrival of the Shrovetide mummers in Act II). As the action unfolds, the threat of excessive gloom is avoided by a characteristically Chekhovian device – 'serious' conversations regularly collapse into bathos and deflation, and 'coherent' discourse is punctuated by 'irrelevances' and tangential *non sequiturs*. This is evident not only in the non-dialogues between Andrei and Ferapont, but also in the continuous stream of random information which Chebutykin imparts from newspapers. The audience readily warms to the Doctor's recipe for falling hair (Act I)[160] and to the snippet that 'Balzac was married in Berdichev' (Act II). All too conscious of our own ignorance, we squirm and sympathise with his Act III confession:

> The day before yesterday they were discussing things at the club; there was talk of Shakespeare and Voltaire... I've never read them, not a single word, but I put on such a knowing look, as if I had. And the others did the same. Oh, how vulgar and vile! (*Poshlost'! Nizost'!*)...[161]

---

in their disparate definitions.

159 Chekhov himself had perpetrated a similarly 'distasteful' joke in a letter of 29 March 1892: 'We have bedbugs and black beetles in plentiful supply. We make them into sandwiches and eat them. Delicious...'. The words *tarakan* (black beetle, cockroach) and *vkusnyi* (delicious) are found in both the letter and the play.

160 An inaccurate prescription, which Olga Knipper had suggested in a letter of 12 September 1900 as a remedy for Chekhov's own incipient baldness.

161 Similarly, in Act I Chebutykin remarks: 'I know, for instance, from the newspapers that there was someone called Dobrolyubov, but what the fellow wrote – I don't know... God alone knows...'. In the first draft, Chebutykin referred to Belinsky, instead of Dobrolyubov (XIII, 275).

The smiles and laughter, both on-stage and in the audience, provide welcome relief from over-solemnity. This delightful pattern of light and shade represents a high-water mark in Chekhov's realism. 'Dialogue' and 'conversations' which at first sight may appear fragmented, haphazard, and even downright nonsensical, actually reflect the essence of daily speech. Chekhov's characters are not eccentric freaks or exclusively 'Russian', and nor are they exceptionally introverted, isolated and uncommunicative. The dramatist perceived that civilised people speak and behave in this way, preoccupied with their own thoughts, hopes, dreams, hurts and griefs, and only half-heeding the corresponding thoughts, hopes, dreams, etc., of those with whom they are supposedly conversing. Sense and nonsense,[162] relevance and irrelevance, profundity and absurdity permeate everyday discourse. Chekhov's humour, characteristically laconic and restrained, is also evident in his correspondence, particularly in his younger years, before he was ravaged by tuberculosis.

Topicality and 'Russianness'

Some early British critics regarded Chekhov and his characters as outlandishly 'Russian', almost as visitors from another planet. In 1938 one reviewer hailed Michel Saint-Denis' production of *Three Sisters* at the Queen's Theatre, while conceding:

> True that the play itself, one hundred per cent. Russian, has a tone alien to our English temperament and ideals.
>
> But it is just that fact which makes the present accomplishment so remarkable. Players and producer, scene designer and costumier, have contrived to fuse into one glorious whole a state of mind and way of living wholly and undeniably of a particular period, a particular country, and a particular place in that country...[163]

It is indeed 'wholly and undeniably' true that *Three Sisters* is a play written by a 'Russian' author at a 'particular' time (1900), and set at that

162 In Act IV Kulygin tells how a pupil mistook the Russian word *chepukha* (nonsense) for a Latin word, *renyxa*. (In Cyrillic script *chepukha* [чепуха] does indeed look like *renyxa*.) The nihilistic Chebutykin later reprises this 'nonsensical' misunderstanding – when Irina is trying to discover what recently happened between Tuzenbakh and Solyony, Chebutykin retorts: 'Renyxa. Chepukha.'

163 Sydney W. Carroll, unidentified cutting, 10 February 1938.

time in a 'particular place' in Russia ('in the chief town of one of the provinces', 'in a county town' [*v gubernskom gorode*], according to Chekhov's instruction beneath the cast list; 'in a provincial town such as Perm', according to his letter to Gorky on 16 October 1900). *Three Sisters* is a 'realistic' piece, and its characters are undoubtedly products of the society and age in which they live.

Readers seeking to approach the text as a source of historical or sociological information are free to see therein a reflection of contemporary Russian society and psychology. It is perfectly possible to regard numerous statements and gestures as politically and socially revealing. The Prozorovs and their friends might, for instance, be interpreted as ineffectual specimens or victims of a moribund class system, which has doomed them to useless inertia and genteel pretentiousness. Tuzenbakh's prophecy of the imminent cleansing storm (Act I) could be taken as a premonition (ardently shared by the author?) of that mighty deliverance, the Great October Socialist Revolution.[164] Similarly, Natasha's take-over of the household may be considered sociologically significant, an indication of the rise of the *petite bourgeoisie*, to replace a decadent upper class.[165]

Yet Chekhov himself would have recoiled from such a simplistic and blinkered analysis. His whole life's experience had led him from slavery to freedom, from dogma to independence, from barbarism to culture. Although by no means indifferent to the welfare of individuals and society, he refused to reduce everything to historical determinism and social categories. 'There will never be any revolution in Russia', he had predicted in a letter of 9 February 1888. Several years later (in his letter to Suvorin on 25 November 1892) he characterised himself and the writers of his generation: 'We have no politics, we don't believe in revolution...'. Early in 1899, when he sold to the Petersburg publisher Adolf Marx (or Marks) the copyright of his entire works, past and future, Chekhov was clearly amused by the coincidence of surname between that publisher and the scourge of capitalism, Karl Marx: 'Having sold my works to Marx, will I be entitled to call myself a Marxist?' (letter of 27 January 1899); 'I've become a Marxist for the rest of my life' (22 February 1899). As for 'real' Marxists, Chekhov made a revealing comment shortly after arriving in Nice, where he completed his revision of *Three Sisters*:

---

164 This was, indeed, the attitude adopted by various Soviet critics (see, for instance, G. Berdnikov, *Chekhov-dramaturg* [Moscow, 1981], p. 241).

165 It is possible to treat *The Cherry Orchard* in this same blunt way, allotting plus or minus signs to Ranevskaya and Gaev (childish landowners), Trofimov (revolutionary prophet), and Lopakhin (businessman, capitalist entrepreneur).

> After Yalta this place seems just like paradise... And in the streets the people are cheerful, noisy, laughing, there's no sign of either a police chief or of Marxists with their sulky physiognomies...
>
> (*To L.V. Sredin*, 26 December 1900 [8 January 1901])

Chekhov saw the problem of human happiness and perfectibility in broader and more subtle terms than anything contained within a Marxist panacea.

Nevertheless, there are several moments in the play where the social criticism voiced by certain characters is closely echoed in the writer's own correspondence. Thus, in Act IV of *Three Sisters*, Andrei pronounces the most devastating judgement upon the provincial Russian town:

> Why, having scarcely begun to live, do we become dull, grey, uninteresting, lazy, indifferent, useless, unhappy?... Our town has been in existence for two hundred years, it has a hundred thousand inhabitants, and there's not one distinguished from all the others, not one hero or saint either in the past or the present, not one scholar, not one artist, nobody remarkable in any way, who might arouse envy or a passionate desire to emulate him... All they do is eat, drink, sleep, and then die... Others are born and they too eat, drink, sleep and then, to avoid being stupefied by boredom, they lend some variety to their lives by indulging in vile gossip, vodka, gambling, malicious litigation, and the wives deceive their husbands, while the husbands tell lies and pretend that they see nothing and hear nothing, and all this invincible vulgarity crushes the children, and the divine spark is extinguished within them, and they become the same miserable, indistinguishable corpses as their mothers and fathers...

Andrei nevertheless finds some consolation in thoughts of a brighter future:

> The present is hateful, but when I think of the future, how good it feels! There's a sense of release and spaciousness; and in the distance a light gleams, I see freedom, I see myself and my children being freed from idleness, from kvass,[166]

166 Kvass (*kvas*) is a fermented beverage, made from rye-flour or bread with malt.

> from roast goose and cabbage, from after-dinner naps, from ignoble parasitism...[167]

Andrei's impassioned speeches reflect the dramatist's own position. Chekhov's letters reveal a lifelong distaste for provincial mediocrity and greyness, whether they be of the Taganrog, Yalta, or Badenweiler variety:

> Just like Asia! Hereabouts[168] is so like Asia, I simply can't believe my own eyes. Sixty thousand inhabitants do nothing but eat, drink and multiply – they have no other interests whatsoever... Not a sign of a newspaper or book... The town is beautifully situated in all respects, the climate is splendid, the fruits of the earth abound – yet the locals are sickeningly inert... There are no patriots, businessmen, poets – or even decent bakers...
>
> (*To N.A. Leikin,* 7 April 1887)

In *Three Sisters*, Natasha – while a 'universal' symbol of small-mindedness – may also be deemed a specifically Russian incarnation of vulgarity (*poshlost'*) and philistinism (*meshchanstvo*).[169] *Poshlost'* is also a prime target in Chekhov's short stories: that vulgarity and complacency which is the very antithesis of sensitivity and spirituality. In his final story, *The Bride*, the heroine Nadya beholds the rooms which she is to inhabit after her marriage, and sees nothing but '*poshlost'*, stupid, naive, intolerable *poshlost'*...'. Chekhov's letters testify to his loathing of *poshlost'* and *meshchanstvo*.[170]

---

167 In an earlier draft, Andrei confides that he wakes up early every morning: 'I think of how, in a couple of years' time, I'll finally lose all my money [or, I'll become completely insolvent], I'll be a pauper, this house will be sold, my wife will leave me – and suddenly my soul feels such a sense of release and spaciousness, and in the distance a light gleams, I have a premonition of freedom, and then I long to flee to my three sisters, to flee to them, to shout out: sisters, I'm saved, I'm saved!' (XIII, 303).

168 After a seven-year absence, Chekhov was revisiting his native town, Taganrog.

169 In Act I Masha refers to Natasha's yellow skirt with its 'vulgar little fringe' (*s etakoi poshlen'koi bakhromoi*), and in Act IV Andrei says of his wife: 'Sometimes she strikes me as amazingly vulgar' (*inogda ona kazhetsia mne udivitel'no poshloi*). In Act II Masha exclaims concerning Natasha: '*Meshchanka!*' (variously translated as 'Petty, vulgar creature!' [Garnett], 'Petty little bourgeois housewife!' [Fen], 'Little shopkeeper!' [Frayn]).

170 'There is nothing more vulgar than the petty-bourgeois life (*Net nichego poshlee meshchanskoi zhizni*)...' (letter of 16 June 1892); 'Philistinism

Another specifically Russian (though not 'topical') aspect of *Three Sisters* is the stream of literary quotations and reminiscences which permeate the play. This is a favourite device of Chekhov, particularly prominent in *The Seagull* (with its echoes of *Hamlet* and Maupassant). Since the milieu is an educated one, it is perhaps scarcely surprising that several authors are mentioned by name, or reference is made to their works. There is no need, however, to exaggerate the importance of the role of literary quotations in *Three Sisters* – Chekhov was not seeking to create some sort of rebus or conundrum, to be savoured and solved by the erudite scholar alone. In *Three Sisters*, life is more important than literature.

The allusions to Russian authors naturally mean more to a native audience than to British readers and theatre-goers, although the full range of reference needs to be explained even to Russians.[171] Literary quotations are deployed by various characters for different ends. If Kulygin's Latin tags (deriving from Cicero, Juvenal, and Pliny 'the Elder') are a natural extension of his pedantic, pedagogic personality, for Solyony the Lermontov pose serves as a mask, to hide or perhaps augment his anxious and tortured psyche.[172] Solyony also readily declaims two menacing lines of comic doggerel, stemming from Krylov's fable *The Peasant and the Workman* (*Krest'ianin i Rabotnik*) (1815), which might be approximately rendered as:

(*meshchanstvo*) is a great evil from the Christian and the economic and every other point of view...' (26 February 1903).

171 The essential literary echoes are listed in XIII, 464-6. Apart from works by Gogol, Griboedov, Krylov, Lermontov and Pushkin, there are snatches of popular song, operetta and opera (in Act III, the enamoured Vershinin sings two lines in praise of love from *Evgeny Onegin*, presumably the Tchaikovsky opera based on Pushkin's novel in verse), Latin quotations (by Kulygin), and a fleeting paraphrase of Shakespeare (when, in Act II, Vershinin's 'Half my life for a glass of tea!' suggests to the Russian ear a translation of Richard III's cry, 'A horse! a horse! my kingdom for a horse!' [*Richard III*, Act V, Scene IV]).

172 In Act II Solyony declares: 'I have something of Lermontov's character. I even look rather like Lermontov...so people say...'. (Concerning this claim, see Chekhov's letter to I.A. Tikhomirov on 14 [27] January 1901, cited in the Introduction.) In Act IV Solyony also quotes, somewhat inaccurately, two restless lines from Lermontov's poem 'The Sail' ('*Parus*') (1832). In general, Solyony awkwardly identifies with the 'Romantic' persona – thus, in Act II, he briefly utters some words spoken by Chatsky in Griboedov's play *Woe from Wit* (*Gore ot uma*) (1823-4), and alludes to Aleko, the lone hero of Pushkin's long poem *The Gypsies* (*Tsygany*) (1824). Aleko, like Solyony, murders through jealous love.

He had no time to say 'Alack!'
Before the bear was on his back.[173]

Two other characters are particularly associated with 'literary' quotations. Chebutykin naturally operates on a lower level, since he admits that, after graduating, 'I've not read even a single book, I've read nothing but newspapers' (Act I). Accordingly, Chebutykin has merely heard of Dobrolyubov (Act I), or Shakespeare and Voltaire (Act III), and – apart from mimicking Solyony's bear-refrain (Act IV) – he confines himself to snatches of comic opera (Act I) and popular song ('Ta-ra-ra-boom-de-ay', Act IV).[174]

The person most hauntingly under the spell of literary quotation is Masha, who remains moodily obsessed for much of the play by the incantatory opening lines of the prologue to Pushkin's long poem *Ruslan and Lyudmila* (1820). They form the first words she utters in Act I:

U lukomor'ia dub zelenyi;
Zlataia tsep' na dube tom...
(By the shores of a bay there is a green oak-tree;
There is a golden chain on that oak...)[175]

Masha repeats these lines towards the end of Act I, and then, compulsively, late in Act IV, just after her final parting from Vershinin. As she does so in

---

173 This closely corresponds to Constance Garnett's translation. The words '*On akhnut' ne uspel, kak na nego medved' nasel*' are spoken by Solyony in Acts I and IV (and mockingly repeated by Chebutykin in Act IV). The obvious 'menacing' aspect of these lines is that they recur shortly before the duel, in which Solyony kills Tuzenbakh. This bear-image has also been linked with the menace of Protopopov. David Magarshack writes that, in Act I, Masha 'seems uncertain about Protopopov's patronymic and, as though still remembering Solyony's quotation, calls him Mikhail Potapych, the humorous name given by Russian peasants to a bear' (*Chekhov the Dramatist* [London, 1952], p. 235). Earlier, a Soviet critic had remarked that Natasha (described by Andrei in Act IV as a 'rough-skinned animal') is a 'worthy partner' of the 'bear', Protopopov (V. Ermilov, *Dramaturgiia Chekhova* [Moscow, 1948], p. 162).

174 Late in Act II, Chebutykin joins Tuzenbakh and Andrei in a brief rendition (song and dance) of the Russian folk-song, '*Akh vy seni, moi seni...*' ('Ah, my porch, my nice new porch...').

175 This is the literal translation by Dimitri Obolensky, in *The Penguin Book of Russian Verse* (Harmondsworth, 1965), p. 96. Masha's Pushkin quotation was an afterthought of Chekhov. In the first draft, she cited a much less poetic dispatch reporting a Russian military victory in 1773: 'Thanks be to God, and thanks be to us, Turtukai has been captured, and we are there...' (*Slava Bogu, slava nam, Turtukai vziat, i my tam...* , XIII, 275, 466).

Act IV, she feels 'I'm going mad', and she begins to mix up the words: 'Green tom-cat...green oak-tree... (*Kot zelenyi...dub zelenyi...*)'. It is true that, in Pushkin's poem, the third and fourth lines (not quoted in *Three Sisters*, but familiar to many Russians) read:

> *I dnem i noch'iu kot uchenyi*
> *Vsë khodit po tsepi krugom...*
> (And day and night a learned cat
> Ceaselessly walks round on the chain...)[176]

There is no need to over-interpret the 'symbolism' of Masha's refrain, although it may be tempting to view Kulygin as the 'learned [tom-] cat', the 'chain' as representing the bonds (wanted or unwanted) of love, and the 'oak-tree' and the 'shores of a bay' as images of natural beauty and freedom (such as Masha before she became attached to Kulygin?).[177]

In Act II Vershinin remarks to Masha:

> A lofty way of thinking is highly characteristic of the Russian, but, tell me, why does he aim so low in everyday life? Why?

Several characters in *Three Sisters* are conscious of their 'Russianness'. Thus, in Act I, Vershinin (rather pretentiously?) praises the healthy 'Russian'[178] climate of the northern provincial town, and Tuzenbakh (Act II) takes pains to convince Irina of his Russian, rather than Germanic, origins.

To generalise about 'national character' seems hazardous, and untypical of Chekhov himself, who had once written: 'I regard signs and labels as mere prejudice' (letter of 4 October 1888). Yet the dramatist was not wholly averse to acknowledging national characteristics. In a lengthy letter of 30 December 1888, he had emphasised the peculiarly 'Russian excitability' of Ivanov (in his play of that name), a quality which 'soon turns to exhaustion', contrasting this aspect of his hero with the perpetual excitability of the

---

176 Again, this is Dimitri Obolensky's translation. The cat is a tom-cat (*kot*).

177 The unhappily married Masha may have spent much of her time reading. In Act II she recalls that 'Gogol said: living on this earth is a bore, my friends!', and, after her Act III 'confession', she declares: 'Now I shall be like Gogol's madman...silence...silence...' (an allusion to Gogol's story, *The Diary of a Madman* [*Zapiski sumasshedshego*], 1835).

178 He actually uses the adjective 'Slavonic' or 'Slav' (*slavianskii klimat*), but this is usually translated as 'Russian climate'.

Frenchman and the total unexcitability of the German.

Sydney W. Carroll may have claimed in 1938 that the play *Three Sisters*, 'one hundred per cent. Russian, has a tone alien to our English temperament and ideals'. Popular British prejudice might maintain that the 'alien' Russian temperament is eccentric and extreme, unpredictably volatile as it swings from frenzied ecstasy to joyless melancholia. Those 'Russians' throw bombs, seek God, confess the darkest sins, cherish the brightest dreams, laugh, love, drink, despair, and die.

Such clichés are essentially ludicrous. In his reserve, restraint, fastidiousness, and habitual understatement, Chekhov the man would seem more 'English' than the English themselves. Moreover, if the preoccupations of the 'Russian' characters in *Three Sisters* have been accurately identified, who is to say that the 'British' are not equally stirred by questions of love, work, happiness, the passage of time, God, and meaning?

Universality

Three Sisters is a work of art, and another book could be written to explore the marvel of Chekhov's artistry, to dissect the beauty of the butterfly. A sympathetic reader or onlooker scarcely needs to have these things explained, since (as Olivier observed) Chekhov's 'intentions, rhythms and scoring are clear to the susceptible initiate'.[179] The action on-stage might appear extremely natural, with seemingly casual comings and goings, and yet there is nothing haphazard or random about this deceptively 'artless' 'slice of life'.

Many people have noted the musicality of Chekhov's drama and prose[180] – the pauses,[181] the sounds, the interplay of sunshine and candlelight,

---

179 Laurence Olivier, in the programme for *Three Sisters* at the National Theatre, London, 1967.

180 In late March 1901 Maxim Gorky wrote to Chekhov: '*Three Sisters* is going splendidly! Better than *Uncle Vanya*. It's music, not acting (*Muzyka, ne igra*)...'. Andrei Belyi remarked: 'The dialogue of *Three Sisters* and *The Cherry Orchard* – yes, that's music!'; 'Chekhov's "mood plays" are musical' (from articles first published in 1907 and 1904 respectively, collected in his book *Arabeski* [Moscow, 1911], pp. 399, 403).

Kenneth MacMillan's ballet *Winter Dreams* (premièred at the Royal Opera House, Covent Garden, on 7 February 1991) was inspired by *Three Sisters*. MacMillan explained that he 'tried to capture the atmosphere and melancholy of Chekhov's masterpiece'. Set to the music of Tchaikovsky and traditional Russian melodies, and performed by the Royal Ballet (including Darcey Bussell as Masha and Irek Mukhamedov as Vershinin), *Winter Dreams* was shown on BBC television on 29 December 1992.

181 In *Three Sisters*, the number of stage directions indicating a pause (*pauza*)

wisdom and silliness, joy and despair, the tension and languor. There is a symmetry, from the opening mention of death, a military band, and a rifle-salute, to the closing pistol-shot and death (off-stage), and the receding strains of a military band. An accordion can be heard off-stage at the beginning and end of Act II; other off-stage sounds include Andrei's violin-playing (Act I), the nurse singing to baby Bobik (Act II), the voices and laughter of the mummers (Act II), the approach of Protopopov's troika with its bells (Act II), the alarm signalling the fire, and the noise of a passing fire-engine (Act III), and the piano rendition of 'The Maiden's Prayer' (Act IV). On-stage, Tuzenbakh quietly plays the piano (Act I), Fedotik may spin his humming-top (Act I), Masha remarks upon the noise in the stove, which reminds her of a sound shortly before Father died (Act II), Fedotik and Rodé sing quietly, to a guitar accompaniment (Act II), Tuzenbakh strums a waltz on the piano (Act II), itinerant musicians (first heard off-stage from afar) play the violin and harp (Act IV). The clock strikes twelve (Act I), and Chebutykin's watch chimes (Act IV).

Three Sisters thus contains a whole musical score, and the director needs to be conductor, choreographer and lighting technician (especially for the candle-lit chiaroscuro of Acts II and III, with the off-stage fire of the third act). All such 'effects' require the subtlest treatment, to avoid that heavy-handed and obtrusive naturalism which Chekhov frequently resented in Stanislavsky's methods. The notoriously elusive Chekhovian 'mood' replaces the climaxes of conventional dramatic action.[182]

Chekhov's characters are human beings first and foremost, individuals and not symbols (even if at times they seem 'symbolised' by significant details, such as Natasha's malevolently snake-like green belt in Act I, or the piano of Irina's heart with its lost key in Act IV).[183] In their preoccupation with the eternal or insoluble questions, they are representatives of 'mankind' rather than narrowly and exclusively 'Russian'.

---

increases with every act, reflecting a steady deceleration from the springtime expectancy of Act I to the autumnal leave-takings of Act IV. The sixty-five explicit references to a 'pause' divide as follows: Act I – eight; Act II – sixteen; Act III – seventeen; Act IV – twenty-four. In this accumulation of pauses, *Three Sisters* is the slowest and saddest play of Chekhov's great quartet (followed by *Uncle Vanya* with some forty-four indications of 'pause').

182 A more traditional dramatist might have given much greater prominence to such 'events' as the Act III fire or the Act IV duel.

183 Similarly, the great shattered bell which, for Masha in Act IV, represents all the unrealised hopes placed upon brother Andrei. If the image of the shattered bell echoes the broken clock of Act III, so the lost key to Irina's piano/heart reprises Andrei's lost cupboard-key late in Act III (see Z. Papernyi, *'Vopreki vsem pravilam...': P'esy i vodevili Chekhova* [Moscow, 1982], p. 177).

It might be tempting to conclude, on the evidence of this play, that Chekhov fully merits his reputation as a 'pessimist'. When the final curtain falls, only Anfisa and Natasha have attained the happiness they seek (a room to die in, and a house to rule in). Yet one should beware of hastily classifying Chekhov as a 'pessimist' or 'cynic'. In a letter to Lidiya Avilova on 6 (18) October 1897 he even claimed to be a 'cheerful person':

> You complain that my main characters are gloomy. Alas, I'm not to blame! That's not how I intend it, and when I'm writing I don't feel that I'm writing gloomily. At all events, when I work I'm always in a good mood. It has been observed that gloomy people, melancholics, always write merrily, whereas the writing of cheerful people makes the reader feel depressed. And I'm a cheerful person (*A ia chelovek zhizneradostnyi*). At least, I've spent the first thirty years of my life without a care in the world, as they say...

At the end of his short story *The Student* (1894) – which Chekhov allegedly named as his 'favourite' work, and a proof that he was not a 'pessimist'[184] – the theological student Ivan Velikopolsky elatedly recognises the unbroken link connecting past and present:

> And a feeling of youth, health, strength – he was only twenty-two years old – and an inexpressibly sweet expectation of happiness, unknown, mysterious happiness gradually took hold of him, and life seemed to him entrancing, wonderful, and full of lofty meaning.[185]

During his farewell meeting with Irina, before walking off-stage, to the duel and death, Tuzenbakh remarks:

---

184 According to I.A. Bunin, *O Chekhove* (New York, 1955), p. 57. One writer, noting the idealistic and religious elements in Chekhov, alongside his awareness of vulgarity (*poshlost'*) and human 'impotence', characterised his outlook as 'optimopessimism, seeing the triumph of evil...but firmly believing in the future victory of good' (S.N. Bulgakov, *Chekhov kak myslitel'* [Moscow, 1910], p. 31).

185 The closing lines of *The Student* appear unusually 'optimistic'. It should, however, be remembered that Chekhov's own position cannot automatically be identified with that of a young theological student, and the ending remains typically ambiguous. 'He was only twenty-two years old' could suggest naivety as well as positive youth, and the writer takes care to indicate that life 'seemed' (only 'seemed'?) 'entrancing, wonderful, and full of lofty meaning' to the student.

> I feel cheerful. It's as if I were seeing these fir-trees, these maples and birches, for the first time in my life, and everything is looking at me with curiosity, and waiting. What beautiful trees, and really, what a beautiful life there should be all around them!
>
> *A shout is heard: 'Halloo! Hop-hop!'*
>
> I must go, it's time... See, that tree is withered up, yet still it sways in the wind with the others. And in the same way, it seems to me that, if I die, I shall still take part in life, somehow or other. Goodbye, my darling... (*He kisses her hands.*)

Thus Tuzenbakh yearns for immortality, to transcend death. And, no matter what may happen, such a longing cannot be extinguished. In this respect, *Three Sisters* is an optimistic piece. It is an artistic statement which transcends time. The three sisters will live on, whereas Natasha is already spiritually dead. The odious sister-in-law proclaims, after the sound of the distant shot but before Tuzenbakh's death is told, that she will have the avenue of fir-trees chopped down, and then the maple. In the eyes of Chekhov himself, who planted trees in Melikhovo and Yalta, and who would gladly have been a professional gardener had he not been a writer,[186] the wanton destruction of trees was an act of barbarous folly.[187] In 'victory', Natasha announces her own defeat.

Of course, the three sisters and Andrei are weak and ineffective in failing to resist Natasha's onslaught. The Prozorovs may sometimes be insensitive or comic, unduly passive or fatalistic. Yet they are pointing in the right direction, and embody a vast spiritual yearning, a longing for the ideal. They are seeking happiness, love, satisfying work, the meaning of life, perhaps faith. Since these goals are so elusive, it is hardly surprising that they fail to achieve them – but the search goes on, and at the end of Act IV the sisters remain determined to live and work and seek. The play's finale is neither tragic nor triumphant, but nor is it overridingly ironic. Notwithstanding the presence of Kulygin, Andrei and Chebutykin, the abiding impression conveyed by the final tableau is of the three sisters grouped together in unity and mutual support – an

---

186 See his letters of 20 February 1900, 6 December 1901, and 17 December 1901.

187 The mindless demolition of trees is opposed by Khrushchov (in *The Wood Demon*) and Astrov (in *Uncle Vanya*), while *The Cherry Orchard* ends to the thud of axe on tree.

archetypal image as unforgettable as Rembrandt's prodigal son enfolded by his forgiving father.[188]

If Chekhov's intention were primarily to mock and expose the inert gentility of young ladies ill-equipped to live in the present and clinging to idle dreams of past and future, *Three Sisters* would scarcely have earned such acclaim on the international stage. A world potentially populated by Protopopovs, Natashas and their offspring would be a dismal place (better, almost, that such progeny indeed be fried in frying-pans!); whereas the realisation of Vershinin's prediction – that there be six, twelve, and eventually a majority of people like the three sisters – might offer hope for the human race. (But, alas, the three sisters are childless. If only Olga could have married Kulygin, and Irina loved Tuzenbakh, and Masha perhaps remained with Vershinin! Ah, if only everyone could 'live happily ever after'...).

A possible clue to Chekhov's sympathies may be found in his choice of names for the three sisters: Olga, Masha and Irina. When he wrote the play, the actress *Olga* Knipper was soon to become his wife; *Masha* was his only sister, on whom he greatly relied; and he had first admired Knipper in 1898 in the role of *Irina*, the Tsar's wife in Alexei Tolstoy's *Tsar Fedor Ioannovich*. ('I attended a rehearsal of *Fed*[*or*] *Ioan*[*novich*]... If I'd stayed in Moscow, I'd have fallen in love with that Irina' [letter of 8 October 1898]).Was his choice of these three names mere coincidence, and would he have bestowed precisely these names on a trio he wished to denigrate?

To experience *Three Sisters*, to understand and feel the play, is to experience 'life' in a heightened and refined form. Amid all the dross, of our own and others' making, true art distils, uplifts, illuminates. Portraying ordinary people in everyday circumstances, *Three Sisters* captures the beauty and the brevity of human life, the blessing and the bewilderment.

In one of his notebooks Chekhov wrote:

> Between 'God exists' and 'there is no God' there lies an entire vast field which a true sage traverses with great difficulty. A Russian knows only one of these two extremes,

---

188 B. Zingerman likens the harmonious image of the three sisters to Andrei Rublev's icon of the *Trinity* (*Teatr Chekhova i ego mirovoe znachenie* [Moscow, 1988], pp. 79-80). The three sisters are alone together on stage on only three brief occasions – at the start of the play, late in Act III, and perhaps towards the end of Act IV (although Chebutykin is hovering in the background).

> but he finds the middle ground between them uninteresting, and he usually knows nothing or very little.[189]

Three Sisters explores the 'middle ground' between hope and despair, happiness and sorrow, love and loneliness, yearning and indifference, culture and *poshlost'*, beautiful trees and strong-smelling flowers, light and dark (the *massa sveta* and the *temnaia massa*), life and death, the ideal and the real.

The gulf between aspiration and achievement inevitably brings grief. The profound sadness which permeates Chekhov's penultimate play is echoed in the mood of his penultimate story, *The Bishop* (1902), on which he was already working when he wrote *Three Sisters*. In a crucial episode in that story, while he is sitting in church, tears flow down the Bishop's face:

> He reflected that he had achieved everything accessible to a man in his position, he was a believer, and yet not everything was clear, there was something still missing, he did not want to die; and it still seemed to him that he lacked something most important of which he had once vaguely dreamed, and that now in the present he was still disturbed by that same hope for the future which he had felt in childhood, and at college and abroad...

The Bishop's basic predicament is one that afflicts any sensitive person capable of aspiring upwards, beyond temporal physical complacency. To be human and mortal means that there is always 'something still missing', whether it be the solace of a religious faith or a linking 'general idea', living contact with one's fellow human beings, or everlasting health and happiness.

Desmond MacCarthy, that most perceptive of critics, recognised in 1938:

> In common with all genuine works of art *The Three Sisters* is addressed to the contemplative, not the practical mind. To the practical the spectacle of failure in any shape is merely depressing; not necessarily to the contemplative, who, whether religious or sceptical, have down the ages found wisdom and even a beauty in the lessons of frustration...
>
> Chekov[190] is the dramatist of good-byes...; good-byes to

---

189 XVII, 33-4; similarly, XVII, 224 (diary note of 1897).

190 That is how MacCarthy spells the writer's name. In the 1910s, 1920s and 1930s his surname was also transliterated as Chehov, Tchehov, Tchekhof, Tchekhoff, Tchekhov, Tchekoff, etc.

> hopes, possessions and ambitions, good-byes to love. And unless in a totalitarian civilisation men become entirely absorbed in incessant production, or their responses so thoroughly 'conditioned' by education that they ask no more than what the State provides (an awful possibility!), human life will continue to be largely a series of farewells concluding with death, the last... Yet out of this conception of life, which the practical optimist would label 'depressing', and the Communist regard as sociologically symptomatic, Chekov makes a work of art which exalts like a beautiful piece of music. It is not in a mood of depression one leaves the theatre after seeing *The Three Sisters*, the best of all his plays...[191]

Stanislavsky recalls Chekhov's unwillingness to 'explain' the meaning of his plays:

> It may seem strange, but he could not talk about his own plays. Feeling as if he were being questioned himself by a judicial examiner, he would grow confused, and in order to find a way out of the strange situation and get rid of us, he would take advantage of his usual statement:
>
> 'Listen, I wrote it down; it is all there.'[192]

It is, indeed, 'all there' – one merely needs eyes to see. Then, literary criticism becomes superfluous.

---

191 Desmond MacCarthy, *The New Statesman and Nation* (5 February 1938), p. 206.

192 Constantin Stanislavsky, *My Life in Art* (London, 1924), p. 361.

Part Two

Literary Criticism

There is nothing unique or sacrosanct about the role of the 'literary critic'. Although Chekhov himself often lamented the lack of decent critics in Russia, anyone (reader, student, scholar, audience, director, actor, reviewer) who approaches *Three Sisters* thoughtfully and sensitively may provide valuable and perceptive insights.

Such is the subtlety, complexity and ambiguity of Chekhov's play that there can be no critical consensus in interpreting the characters of Vershinin, Tuzenbakh, the three sisters and Andrei, or in evaluating the vexed question of the author's pessimism or optimism, his involvement or detachment, idealism or irony. Perhaps it is inevitable that judgements are frequently fuelled by personal prejudice or preference. In a very real way, one's response to this play is a measure of one's attitude to life itself.

The critical literature about *Three Sisters* is virtually inexhaustible.[1] A variety of opinions will be considered in this section.

Russian-language Criticism

Among the first people to respond to *Three Sisters*, and to Chekhov's drama in general, were a number of leading poets and writers. An early Russian comment on *Three Sisters* is found in English translation in the London journal *The Athenaeum*. Here the Symbolist Valerii Briusov declared:

> Every new production of Chekhov is an event in the literary world. During the past year his drama 'The Three Sisters'... has appeared. In his usual masterly way he represents in it all the terror, all the helplessness of Russian town life... The actors torment each other; all loathe themselves, and know that there is no way of extricating themselves from their position...[2]

1 See entries in the Bibliography under Lantz, Meister, Proffer and Sendich.

2 Valerii Briusov, in *The Athenaeum* 3847 (20 July 1901), p. 86. Briusov generally felt cool towards Chekhov's realism (see *Literaturnoe nasledstvo*,

Leonid Andreev (1901) was moved to tears by a performance of the play, and filled with a tremendous desire to live. Rejecting the view that *Three Sisters* is a 'deeply pessimistic work', Andreev identified its 'basic tragic melody' as a mighty 'longing to live', an urgent call 'to life, freedom and happiness!'.[3]

The Marxist Anatoly Lunacharsky (1903) expressed a total lack of sympathy for the elegant, privileged, languorous three sisters. Utterly unimpressed by their 'beautiful clothes and faces' and their tearful dream of Moscow, Lunacharsky advocated instead an active 'struggle' for the real 'radiant, beautiful life'.[4]

In various articles of 1904 and 1907 the Symbolist Andrei Belyi recognised Chekhov as an 'amazing stylist', a 'realistic artist' who had 'exhausted realism' and thereby arrived at a kind of synthesis of realism and symbolism.[5]

The Symbolist Dmitry Merezhkovsky (1905) emphasised the boredom and dejection of Chekhov's characters, and the pervasive scepticism of the author himself. According to Merezhkovsky, in Chekhov's 'last and perhaps greatest works', *Three Sisters* and *The Cherry Orchard*, 'all the characters seem to have died long ago', and continue to live by inertia, while emitting a stench of decay. To the religious philosopher Merezhkovsky, Chekhov's failure to espouse a faith or a linking idea was tantamount to nihilistic godlessness.[6]

An even more 'negative' view of Chekhov's entire creation was expounded by Lev Shestov (1905). While concentrating particularly on certain stories, Shestov distortedly maintained:

> Chekhov was a singer of hopelessness... He killed human hopes... Art, science, love, inspiration, ideals, the future – ... once Chekhov has touched them immediately fade, wither and die... In Chekhov's hands everything died...
>
> The only real Chekhovian hero is the hopeless man... Creation out of nothing! (*Tvorchestvo iz nichego!*)...[7]

LXXXV: *Valerii Briusov* [Moscow, 1976], pp. 182, 198).

3 Leonid Andreev, in *Polnoe sobranie sochinenii Leonida Andreeva* VI (St Petersburg, 1913), pp. 321-5. Andreev's reflections had first appeared in October 1901, under the pseudonym James Lynch.

4 A.V. Lunacharsky, 'O khudozhnike voobshche i nekotorykh khudozhnikakh v chastnosti', *Russkaia mysl'* 2 (1903), pp. 59, 60.

5 See especially 'A.P. Chekhov' (1907) and '"Vishnevyi sad"' (1904), in Andrei Belyi, *Arabeski* (Moscow, 1911), pp. 395-405.

6 See D.S. Merezhkovsky, *Chekhov i Gor'kii* (St Petersburg, 1906), pp. 17, 56-67 (article first published in 1905).

7 Lev Shestov, 'Tvorchestvo iz nichego (A.P. Chekhov)', in his book *Nachala*

In the course of an affectionate memoir, Maxim Gorky (1905) commented upon Olga's inability to find a single 'powerful word of protest against vulgarity (*poshlost'*)' and upon Vershinin's failure to notice that, 'out of boredom and stupidity', Solyony is quite prepared to kill the 'pathetic' Baron Tuzenbakh. The energetic and revolutionary-minded Gorky regarded Chekhov's 'impotent' characters (dreamy 'slaves') with unmistakable impatience.[8]

The poet and playwright Innokenty Annensky (1906) offered an emotional and elegantly expressed response to the main characters in *Three Sisters*, whom he regarded as '*literary* people' reflecting various aspects of the Russian soul (and of Annensky himself). This sensitive and subjective article, which at first seems highly sympathetic to the characters' plight, becomes increasingly critical of their dreaminess and indifference (features particularly evident in the men): 'Tomorrow, tomorrow... Moscow... Three hundred years...'[9] In a private letter dated 5 June 1905, Annensky condemned Chekhov's 'dry mind': 'I don't like Chekhov and I'll probably burn my article about *Three Sisters*...'[10]

Kornei Chukovsky (1908), in a refreshingly 'unscholarly' and paradoxical article, noted Chekhov's lifelong antipathy for purposeful, resolute characters (such as Doctor Lvov, Professor Serebryakov, Natasha and Lopakhin), and his sympathy for those who are lost and confused (Ivanov, Uncle Vanya, the three sisters, Ranevskaya and Gaev). Chekhov's dislike of business or busyness (*delo*) and of utilitarianism forms part of his 'religious attitude to life'.[11]

In his lyrical reflections 'Chekhov and Christianity' (1910), Chukovsky emphasised the religious dimension to *Three Sisters* – the sisters and their house are 'holy', while Natasha 'blasphemes' and 'commits sacrilege'. Alluding to the Beatitudes, Chukovsky maintained that Chekhov favours and blesses 'the meek' and 'the poor in spirit'. After seeing *Three Sisters*, Chukovsky smiled and felt forgiven, 'and I realised...that the play was not at all sad, for would I have smiled had it been a sad play?'.[12]

---

i kontsy (St Petersburg, 1908), pp. 3, 5, 6, 32, 39, 40 (article first published, 1905). The title 'Tvorchestvo iz nichego' is sometimes rendered as 'Creation from the Void'.

8 See Maxim Gorky, 'A.P. Chekhov' (words first published in 1905), in *M. Gor'kii i A. Chekhov: Perepiska. Stat'i. Vyskazyvaniia*, compiled by N.I. Gitovich (Moscow, 1951), pp. 138-9.

9 See I.F. Annensky, 'Drama nastroeniia: Tri sestry', in his *Kniga otrazhenii* (St Petersburg, 1906), pp. 147-67.

10 Quoted in Innokenty Annensky, *Knigi otrazhenii* (Moscow, 1979), p. 460.

11 See K. Chukovsky, *Ot Chekhova do nashikh dnei: Literaturnye portrety. Kharakteristiki* (St Petersburg and Moscow, 1908), pp. 1-17.

12 K. Chukovsky, 'Chekhov i khristianstvo', *Mir* 5 (1910), pp. 356-9. Much later,

On 12 April 1909, the Symbolist poet Alexander Blok felt 'absolutely shattered' after seeing *Three Sisters* performed by the Moscow Arts Theatre company in Petersburg. The next day, he described his impressions in a letter to his mother: 'I accepted Chekhov in his entirety, as he is, into the pantheon of my soul, and I shared his tears, his grief and humiliation...'.[13]

In a wide-ranging and profoundly sympathetic survey of Chekhov's work, Yuly Aikhenvald (1911) paid tribute to the 'moral beauty' of the three sisters, and recognised in the meditative Vershinin an 'aristocrat of the spirit'. Chekhov is not a 'pessimist' – he is a 'writer of the ideal' (*pisatel' ideala*).[14]

The iconoclastic Futurist Vladimir Mayakovsky (1914) derided those who labelled Chekhov as a 'bard of twilight' or 'protector of the insulted and injured',[15] turning him into a 'nanny and wet-nurse to all these forgotten Firses, men in cases, those who moan: "to Mosco-o-ow"...'.[16] Instead, Mayakovsky proclaimed Chekhov to be one of the 'Kings of the Word', a 'powerful, cheerful artist of the word'.[17]

During the years of turmoil following the Bolshevik revolution of October 1917, when Russians experienced civil war, famine, political terror and the dawn of a 'new age', it is scarcely surprising that Chekhov's plays (allegedly peopled by 'bourgeois' or 'petty-bourgeois' characters with their idle dreams and aspirations) now appeared in a new historical light.

---

publishing in the atheistic Soviet Union, Chukovsky drastically amended this religious view. He claimed that Chekhov 'scarcely sought to glorify' such characters as the three sisters, although Chekhov was attracted by the fact that they were 'martyrs' – 'martyrs of their own flabbiness, passivity, spiritual impoverishment, and weak will' (Kornei Chukovsky, *O Chekhove* [Moscow, 1967], p. 155).

13 Alexander Blok, *Sobranie sochinenii v vos'mi tomakh* VIII (Moscow-Leningrad, 1963), p. 281.

14 Yu. Aikhenvald, *Siluety russkikh pisatelei: Vypusk I* (Moscow, 1911), pp. 248, 256, 260, 264.

15 An allusion to Dostoevsky's novel, *The Insulted and Injured* (*Unizhennye i oskorblennye*) (1861).

16 Firs is the aged manservant, left behind at the end of *The Cherry Orchard*; *The Man in a Case* is a famous story of 1898; and 'those who moan: "to Mosco-o-ow"...' are mainly the three sisters.

17 See Vladimir Mayakovsky, 'Dva Chekhova' (1914), in his *Polnoe sobranie sochinenii v trinadtsati tomakh* I (Moscow, 1955), pp. 294-301. For further disdainful references to *Three Sisters* and the longing for Moscow, see elsewhere in this thirteen-volume edition: III, 123; IX, 13, 437-8; XII, 272; XIII, 118.

In 1919 the theatre historian Nikolai Efros published a detailed and sympathetic account of the 1901 Moscow Arts Theatre production.[18]

M. Grigorev (1924) rather prosaically identified the main themes of *Three Sisters*, and various aspects of Chekhov's dramatic method, before concluding that his plays 'belong mainly to the very end of the last century' and rarely move the 'new spectator' to tears.[19]

In 1926 Konstantin Stanislavsky indicated the universality of Chekhov's fundamental theme:

> Chekhov is inexhaustible because, despite the commonplace uneventfulness which he seems perpetually to depict, he always speaks, in his basic spiritual leitmotif, not of the random or particular, but of the Human with a capital letter...
>
> All this is from the realm of the eternal, which we cannot regard without deep emotion...[20]

S.D. Balukhatyi (1927) subjected *Three Sisters* to a meticulous formal analysis, noting Chekhov's 'impressionistic' manner of writing, his use of pauses to intensify the 'lyrical expressiveness' of various speeches, the gradual slowing of the play's tempo as its tone moves from major to minor, and its psychological and social aspects.[21]

A. Derman (1929) claimed that, although the first post-revolutionary years had witnessed a temporary decline of interest in Chekhov's life and works, there were now signs of an undoubted revival.[22]

Writing outside the Soviet Union, M. Kurdyumov (1934) examined Chekhov's works, including *Three Sisters*, in an attempt to establish his attitude to life, death, suffering, meaning and religion. Kurdyumov tentatively concluded that Chekhov was not a 'convinced atheist', and was indeed a 'Christian' in his immense love and compassion for his fellow-man.[23]

By 1936, at the time of the Stalin terror, S. Balukhatyi felt obliged to

---

18 Nikolai Efros, *'Tri sestry': P'esa A.P. Chekhova v postanovke Moskovskogo Khudozhestvennogo teatra*, foreword by Vl. Nemirovich-Danchenko (Petersburg, 1919).

19 M. Grigorev, *Stsenicheskaia kompozitsiia chekhovskikh p'es* (Moscow, 1924), pp. 120-3.

20 K.S. Stanislavsky, *Moia zhizn' v iskusstve* (Moscow, 1926), p. 292.

21 S. Balukhatyi, *Problemy dramaturgicheskogo analiza: Chekhov* (Leningrad, 1927), especially pp. 120-47.

22 A. Derman, *Tvorcheskii portret Chekhova* (Moscow, 1929), pp. 9-12.

23 See M. Kurdyumov, *Serdtse smiatennoe: O tvorchestve A.P. Chekhova. 1904-1934* (Paris, 1934), pp. 134, 148-9, 205.

politicise his appreciation of *Three Sisters*, adding obligatory references to Lenin and the growth of the revolutionary movement, and emphasising the negative critical reaction in 1901 to the pessimism and hopelessness of the play's characters and mood. Balukhatyi now gave simplistic Marxist labels to Chekhov's complex characters ('representatives of the bourgeois intelligentsia...'). While acknowledging the aesthetic and historical value of Chekhov's plays, Balukhatyi demonstrated his loyalty as a Soviet citizen by offering a shallow generalisation:

> We, who are cut off from the terrible period of the 'Chekhov era' by the dividing-line of the Socialist Revolution, – we, who are living through the first years of Socialist construction, – cannot be keenly affected or deeply moved by the griefs, sufferings and hopes of people belonging to the past. We may 'sympathise' with them, but we cannot share in their misfortunes...[24]

A. Derman (1939) exposed the 'fallaciousness' of Balukhatyi's argument, by pointing out that the 'dividing-line of the Socialist Revolution' had separated the Russians of today 'not only from Chekhov, but from the entire culture of the past'. Derman convincingly remarked that great writers of the past illuminate the innermost recesses of the human heart, portraying passions such as 'love, hate, heroism, fear, rapture, grief, jealousy, avarice, sorrow, joy, etc., etc.' – and therefore Russians still need 'the three sisters yearning for Moscow'.[25]

Nemirovich-Danchenko's revival of *Three Sisters* at the Moscow Arts Theatre in 1940 seems to have confirmed the veracity of Derman's claim. This major Soviet production was painstakingly chronicled by A. Roskin (1946).[26]

V. Ermilov (1944) emphasised the need for 'practical struggle'. As for the beautiful dream of the future, the 'Russian democrat' Chekhov revealed the comic 'disparity between the grandeur of the dream and the weakness of the dreamers'. Ermilov concluded his book (written during the Second World War) with a hymn to the 'heroic Party of Lenin and Stalin': 'The whole of our unbounded country is being transformed into

---

24 S. Balukhatyi, *Chekhov dramaturg* (Leningrad, 1936), pp. 180-1, 287-8.

25 A. Derman, *Anton Pavlovich Chekhov: Kritiko-biograficheskii ocherk* (Moscow, 1939), pp. 206-7, 209-10.

26 A. Roskin, *'Tri sestry' na stsene Khudozhestvennogo teatra* (Leningrad-Moscow, 1946). See also A. Roskin, *A.P. Chekhov: Stat'i i ocherki* (Moscow, 1959).

a blossoming orchard, and the laws of its life have become the laws of truth and beauty...'.[27]

In 1948 Ermilov discussed *Three Sisters* at length, making many reasonable comments while basically seeing the play in narrowly political terms. As a Marxist critic, Ermilov expressed disapproval of Chekhov's 'petty-bourgeois limitations', contrasting his 'separation from the proletarian revolutionary movement' with Gorky's active, 'progressive' commitment. Ermilov alluded to the play's 'sad humour':

> Its characters are incapable of struggle, of action, that is, of real drama. They are capable only of dreaming about a better future... While admiring the sisters' beauty and loving them tenderly, Chekhov smiles sorrowfully at their helplessness, their utter alienation from real life...

Having endured twenty years of Stalinism, Ermilov proposed a positive alternative to Chekhov's characters – 'our Soviet intelligentsia, with its sense of responsibility to the people, with its awareness of its own necessity and usefulness...'.[28]

A. Skaftymov (1948) perceptively analysed the 'principles of the construction' of Chekhov's plays. Whereas pre-Chekhovian, eventful drama typically dealt with one specific vice, evil or obstacle whose removal would enable the characters to be happy, Chekhov portrays habitual, long-lasting grief and dissatisfaction, which lie deeply ingrained in the characters as they experience 'ordinary, grey, monochrome, everyday' existence. Chekhov's characters cherish the poetic dream of a transformed and better life. Although upsurges of hope inevitably give way to further disillusionment, the finale always combines sorrow with 'a passionate dream and faith in the future'. Skaftymov remains refreshingly free from Marxist terminology, except, perhaps, when he seeks to establish a direct or causal link between the characters' frustration and the socio-political stagnation of those times.[29]

---

27 See V. Ermilov, *A.P. Chekhov: Tvorcheskii portret* (Moscow, 1944), especially pp. 32-5, 85-9, 109.

28 V. Ermilov, *Dramaturgiia Chekhova* (Moscow, 1948), pp. 154, 161, 170. In a subsequent study (*A.P. Chekhov* [Moscow, 1954]), V. Ermilov continued his politicisation of Chekhov as a harbinger of revolution. This book also appeared in an English translation – see Vladimir Yermilov, *Anton Pavlovich Chekhov 1860-1904* (Moscow, no date [1956?]).

29 See A. Skaftymov, 'K voprosu o printsipakh postroeniia p′es A.P. Chekhova', in his *Nravstvennye iskaniia russkikh pisatelei* (Moscow, 1972), pp. 404-35 (reflections first published in 1948).

In the closing years of Stalin's reign, G.P. Berdnikov (1950) maintained that the society depicted in *Three Sisters* was 'anti-human' in essence, that Andrei ('a flabby, worthless person') deserves no sympathy, and that the plight of the three sisters degenerates into 'a tragicomedy of weak, virtually useless people'.[30] Berdnikov dismissed Vershinin's 'futile' or 'fruitless' philosophising,[31] and his 'gradualist' theory of progress.[32] Berdnikov continued to expound his socio-political interpretation of the play's themes into the 1980s.

Boris Zaitsev (1954), publishing outside Russia, sensed a certain artificiality in the play, and a 'coolness' or 'chill' (*kholodok*) particularly in Irina, Vershinin, and Tuzenbakh. Zaitsev remained totally unconvinced by the optimistic predictions of these characters: 'Chekhov was no prophet, and one simply cannot believe Tuzenbakh.'[33]

M. Stroeva (1955) offered detailed accounts of the Moscow Arts Theatre productions of *Three Sisters* in 1901 and 1940. Stroeva's interpretation of the play and the productions is heavily politicised, leaning towards an 'optimistic' and 'active' reading. Her critical vocabulary is peppered with Marxist clichés, such as 'reactionary', 'bourgeois', 'revolutionary', 'progressive', 'struggle' and 'protest'.[34]

G.A. Bialyi (1956) condemned the characters' passivity, while recognising that they 'sensitively understand one another', since they are all 'thinking of the same thing – the meaning of life...'.[35] In 1981 Bialyi noted the 'spiritual community' of the three sisters, whom 'one begins to perceive as a single character, despite all their individual uniqueness'.[36]

Sergei Zalygin (1969) offered some idiosyncratic reflections on *Three Sisters* as a play full of 'events' and 'triangles', and on Solyony as a character who is stupid and beyond morality.[37]

Over the past thirty years various critics working in the Soviet Union

---

30 G.P. Berdnikov, *Anton Pavlovich Chekhov: 1860-1904* (Moscow-Leningrad, 1950), pp. 129, 140, 144.

31 Ibid., pp. 135-7.

32 G. Berdnikov, *A.P. Chekhov: Ideinye i tvorcheskie iskaniia* (Leningrad, 1970), pp. 458-61.

33 Boris Zaitsev, *Chekhov: Literaturnaia biografiia* (New York, 1954), pp. 219-20.

34 M. Stroeva, *Chekhov i Khudozhestvennyi teatr: Rabota K.S. Stanislavskogo i Vl.I. Nemirovicha-Danchenko nad p'esami A.P. Chekhova* (Moscow, 1955), especially pp. 102-52 and 253-303.

35 G.A. Bialyi, 'Chekhov', in *Istoriia russkoi literatury* IX, 2 (Moscow-Leningrad, 1956), pp. 414, 416.

36 G. Bialyi, *Chekhov i russkii realizm: Ocherki* (Leningrad, 1981), p. 92.

37 Sergei Zalygin, 'Moi poet' (article first published, 1969), in, for instance, his *Literaturnye zaboty* (Moscow, 1982), pp. 406-11, 416-25.

have written sensitively, knowledgeably and undogmatically about *Three Sisters*. The bibliography lists many valuable works by scholars such as A.P. Chudakov, V.B. Kataev, V.Ia. Lakshin, Z.S. Papernyi, T.K. Shakh-Azizova, A. Turkov and B. Zingerman.

English-language Criticism

A play which is now so familiar to British readers and audiences caused considerable consternation in the first decades of this century. Chekhov's gentle and subtle 'realism', his lyrical 'impressionism' and atmospheric 'plotlessness' took the uninitiated by surprise, provoking bewilderment and patronising scorn.[38]

William Gerhardi's pioneering critical study *Anton Chehov* (1923) remains one of the most perceptive and sympathetic accounts of the writer's art. Gerhardi understood the essence of Chekhov, and of his 'crowning work, the *Three Sisters*':[39]

> Chehov, though the melancholy beauty of his plays and stories is the melancholy of a transitory world, cannot be called a pessimist... Chehov was neither pessimist nor optimist. To him life is neither horrible nor happy, but unique, strange, fleeting, beautiful and awful...
>
> There is a tragic beauty about the three sisters, for they are too fine, too exquisitely sensitive for personal happiness. They go on working humbly, teaching with success, serving the purpose of the future happiness of mankind as much as lies in them to serve, and destined to die with their longings unsatisfied...
>
> There is behind it all a quite exceptional gift of love and sympathy...[40]

Constantin (Konstantin) Stanislavsky's *My Life in Art* appeared in English translation in 1924. Stanislavsky recalled the Moscow Arts Theatre production of 1901 through a filter of historical and political hindsight:

---

38 See, for instance, *Chekhov: The Critical Heritage*, edited by Victor Emeljanow (London, Boston and Henley, 1981).

39 William Gerhardi, *Anton Chehov: A Critical Study* (London, 1923), p. 37.

40 Ibid., pp. 20-2, 186, 153. In 1922 William Gerhardi [Gerhardie] had published his first novel, *Futility*, subtitled 'A Novel on Russian Themes'. Part I, entitled 'The Three Sisters', contains a description (in Chapter II) of a visit to the theatre to see Chekhov's *Three Sisters*. A later passage (Part III, Chapter X) uncannily echoes the Chekhovian theme of waiting.

> The men of Chekhov do not bathe, as we did at that time, in their own sorrow. Just the opposite; they, like Chekhov himself, seek life, joy, laughter, courage. The men and women of Chekhov want to live and not to die... It is not their fault that Russian life kills initiative and the best of beginnings and interferes with the free action and life of men and women...[41]

Throughout the 1920s Prince D.S. Mirsky displayed a somewhat cool, and often unperceptive, attitude towards Chekhov, while recognising that he was 'the greatest writer of his age and of his class':

> This period is the age of Chekhov, and the dominant mood of his work is that which dominates the period. It is one of impotent yearning after something better, like the Three Sisters' yearning after Moscow...
>
> All his characters may really be reduced to two types: the gentle and ineffective dreamer, and the vulgar and efficient man of action... For every foolishness and every absurdity Chekhov has an immense treasure of sympathetic pity and understanding, but not for success...[42]

In 1937 Princess Nina Andronikova Toumanova interpreted *Three Sisters* ('the gloomiest of his plays'), and its ending, in a decidedly autumnal light.[43]

Ronald Peacock (1946) commented sympathetically on Chekhov's typically moral and spiritual preoccupations:

> Chehov is a great idealist. His sentiment, his humour, his satire, his humanity, his form, his poetry, spring from this central fact...
>
> There are no 'moral problems' in Chehov's work as in Ibsen and his disciples; but everywhere there is moral aspiration...[44]

---

41 Constantin Stanislavsky, *My Life in Art*, translated by J.J. Robbins (Boston and London, 1924), pp. 373-4.

42 Prince D.S. Mirsky, *Modern Russian Literature* (London, 1925; reprinted, New York, 1974), pp. 85, 88. See also D.S. Mirsky, 'Chekhov and the English', *The Monthly Criterion* VI, 4 (October 1927), p. 298.

43 See Princess Nina Andronikova Toumanova, *Anton Chekhov: The Voice of Twilight Russia* (New York, 1937; reprinted, 1960), pp. 179, 184, 188.

44 Ronald Peacock, *The Poet in the Theatre* (London, 1946), pp. 82-3.

W.H. Bruford (1947) noted the specifically national and sociological aspects of *Three Sisters*, while also recognising the spiritual or religious dimension to Chekhov's outlook and art.[45]

David Magarshack (1952) regarded *Three Sisters* as a 'play of indirect action', with a strong 'chorus element'. If at times extreme in his judgements (labelling Solyony a 'typical fascist', and Chebutykin an 'idiot' by Act IV), and occasionally inaccurate (claiming that 'Act II begins about nine months after the end of Act I', and that 'Natasha bears Protopopov a child between Act III and Act IV'), Magarshack nevertheless convincingly asserts: 'It is a play which deals with the inmost mysteries of man's soul, the purpose of man's existence, and the ultimate values of life.'[46]

Robert Brustein (1965) rather overemphasises the 'bleakness' of Chekhov's vision in *Three Sisters*, while acknowledging his profound 'humanity'.[47]

Maurice Valency (1966) commented, somewhat harshly, on the role of Moscow ('an opiate which reduces life to a dream'). More sympathetically, Valency continues:

> *The Three Sisters* is Chekhov's masterpiece, the flower of impressionism in the drama. No play has ever conveyed more subtly the sense of the transitory nature of human life, the sadness and beauty of the passing moment...
>
> Vershinin evidently speaks for Chekhov, and his views are clear. But Chebutykin also speaks for Chekhov, and his views are equally clear... The indeterminate area between faith and skepticism measures the extent of Chekhov's spiritual discomfort. Vershinin speaks for his faith; Chebutykin, for his doubt...[48]

Lionel Trilling (1967) responded sensitively to the play and its characters:

> *Three Sisters* is surely one of the saddest works in all literature. It is also one of the most saddening... The frustration and hopelessness to which the persons of the drama fall prey seems to be not only their doom but ours as well...[49]

---

45 See W.H. Bruford, *Chekhov and his Russia: A Sociological Study* (London, 1947), pp. 124-5, 128-9, 206, 209-13.

46 David Magarshack, *Chekhov the Dramatist* (London, 1952), p. 226; other details cited are on pp. 226, 233, 238, 245, 259.

47 See Robert Brustein, *The Theatre of Revolt* (London, 1965), pp. 157-8, 161-2, 166, 178-9.

48 Maurice Valency, *The Breaking String* (New York, 1966), pp. 214, 219, 243.

49 Lionel Trilling, *Prefaces to the Experience of Literature* (New York and

Walter Kerr (1967) noted that 'Chekhov called his principal plays comedies':

> That Chekhov's major plays have gone on being performed as tragedies, or near-tragedies, is well known... If we read him wrong it is because we are reluctant to see our own seriousness – our own intellectuality – parodied. Comedy cuts too close to the bone here, touching us in our pride, affronting our freedom, whipping out from under us the dignity that makes us tragic...[50]

In his detailed commentary, J.L. Styan (1971) adopts a stance of sympathetic detachment towards the three sisters and the entire play. Styan reiterates a view he first expressed in 1960: 'Is this a play of hope? Rather, of resignation and endurance.'[51]

Logan Speirs (1971) offers a chain of dubious and misdirected assertions ('Chekhov sees why potential old maids have always been a standing joke...').[52] Whereas Speirs maintains that Tuzenbakh is 'really the most original thinker among them',[53] David Magarshack (1972) over-readily identifies Chekhov's views with those of Vershinin, and tends to idealise that philosophising soldier.[54]

Harvey Pitcher (1973) achieves one of the most perceptive and sympathetic analyses of *Three Sisters*, emphasising the play's rich emotional content.[55] The only major shortcoming in Pitcher's admirable study is his over-emphasis on the 'emotional', to the virtual exclusion of the 'spiritual' dimension.

Simon Karlinsky (1973) praised *Three Sisters*, while linking it thematically with Chekhov's story *In the Ravine* (*V ovrage*) (1900).[56]

Richard Gilman (1974) provides an outstandingly sensitive and lucid appreciation of Chekhov's play:

London, 1979; first published 1967), p. 28.

50 Walter Kerr, *Tragedy and Comedy* (New York, 1967; London, 1968), pp. 234-5.

51 See J.L. Styan, *Chekhov in Performance: A Commentary on the Major Plays* (Cambridge, 1971), pp. 151-2, 163, 236; also J.L. Styan, *The Elements of Drama* (Cambridge, 1960), p. 207.

52 Logan Speirs, *Tolstoy and Chekhov* (Cambridge, 1971), p. 211.

53 Ibid., p. 207.

54 David Magarshack, *The Real Chekhov* (London, 1972), pp. 126, 136.

55 Harvey Pitcher, *The Chekhov Play: A New Interpretation* (London, 1973).

56 Simon Karlinsky, in *Letters of Anton Chekhov* (New York and London, 1973), pp. 386-7, 323. In Chekhov's story *In the Ravine*, the snake-like, 'naive' Aksinya is a usurper-figure, rather akin to Natasha in *Three Sisters*.

> It would be hard to find a play to equal *The Three Sisters* in its noble austerity and brave acceptances. Loss after loss after loss...and survival at the end...[57]

Donald Rayfield (1975) commented that, although *Three Sisters* 'is one of Chekhov's most symbolic and complex works, it is also his most direct and most emotional treatment of life...'[58]

Beverly Hahn (1977), while basically sympathetic towards the three sisters, nevertheless emphasised their 'passivity' and 'defeatism', and Chekhov's alleged depiction of 'a society in a state of crisis'.[59] It might be countered that no amount of 'activity' can ensure happiness, love, satisfying work, and meaning, and that the play portrays a spiritual and moral quest rather than 'a sense of social crisis'.

The ill-informed remarks of Jesse V. Clardy and Betty S. Clardy (1980) are comically naive and inaccurate.[60]

Chapters on *Three Sisters* continue to appear in many studies of modern drama written by non-Slavists. Ignorance of the Russian language and of Russian-language criticism not infrequently leads to superficial and unwarranted pronouncements. Thus, Timothy J. Wiles (1980) makes a whole series of dubious assertions.[61]

John Tulloch (1980) adopted a narrowly sociological approach, deploying unChekhovian terminology to describe the sisters' 'party world', the 'degraded world' embodied by Natasha, and Vershinin's 'epic vision'. Particularly unconvincing is the suggestion that Vershinin displays a 'scientific vision'.[62]

Michael Frayn (1983) sensibly cautions against identifying any of the characters' views with those of the author, but himself clearly inclines towards an ironic interpretation of the drama.[63]

---

57 Richard Gilman, *The Making of Modern Drama* (New York, 1974), p. 156.

58 Donald Rayfield, *Chekhov: The Evolution of his Art* (London, 1975), p. 211. Donald Rayfield later claimed that 'the whole situation and plot' of *Three Sisters* 'mimics that of *The Geisha* (1896) by Sidney Jones', of which a Russian translation had appeared in 1898 ('Chekhov and Popular Culture', *Irish Slavonic Studies* 9 [1988], pp. 57-8).

59 See Beverly Hahn, *Chekhov: A Study of the Major Stories and Plays* (Cambridge, 1977), pp. 290, 295, 296.

60 Jesse V. Clardy and Betty S. Clardy, *The Superfluous Man in Russian Letters* (Washington, 1980), pp. 87-90.

61 See Timothy J. Wiles, *The Theater Event: Modern Theories of Performance* (Chicago and London, 1980), pp. 37-65.

62 John Tulloch, *Chekhov: A Structuralist Study* (London, 1980), pp. 172-4, 176-7, 182.

63 Michael Frayn, Introduction to his translation of *Three Sisters* (London and

Richard Peace (1983) emphasises the literary aspects of the play, paying particular attention to the role of literary quotation. He claims: 'All the characters suffer from an unwillingness to listen'.[64]

Martin Esslin (1985) recognised Chekhov as a pioneer of various aspects of contemporary drama, including 'the emergence of the *tragicomic* as its prevailing mode':

> There is only a small step from Chekhov's images of a society deprived of purpose and direction to the far more emphatic presentation of a world deprived of its 'metaphysical dimension' in the plays of Beckett, Genet, Adamov, or Ionesco. Admittedly, the dramatists of the Absurd have left the solid ground of reality behind and have taken off into dreamlike imagery and hallucinatory metaphor. Yet it can be argued that Chekhov himself, by his very realism, blazed even that trail. In creating so convincing a picture of the randomness and ambivalence of reality, he, more than any other dramatist before him, opened up the question about the nature of reality itself...[65]

Laurence Senelick (1985) offers a perversely unsympathetic interpretation of *Three Sisters*, blackening the Prozorovs and the soldiers at every opportunity. These characters, so human in their vulnerability and fallibility, so forgivable in their occasional absurdity, and so admirable in their good-naturedness and spiritual aspirations, are dismissed by Senelick as despicable, feckless, pseudo-cultured, pseudo-sensitive, and detached from real values.[66]

New York, 1983), pp. viii-xvi.

64 Richard Peace, *Chekhov: A Study of the Four Major Plays* (New Haven and London, 1983), p. 95. In 1987 Richard Peace again underlined the importance of 'literary allusion' in *Three Sisters*, drawing parallels with both classical Greek theatre and Maeterlinck. Dubiously, he asserted that the sisters are essentially 'blind': 'There is irony...in the surname which Chekhov has given his sisters, for *Prozorov* is from the same root as Merezhkovsky's *prozrevavshiy* "having seen through" (cf. *prozorlivyy* – "perspicacious"). For all the implications of their name, the sisters are blind to what is going on around them... The motif of "three sisters" who are also blind is a symbolic theme found in the poetry of Maeterlinck. In his *Quinze chansons* (Fifteen Songs) of 1896 there are two poems entitled: "Les Trois Sœurs aveugles" (The Three Blind Sisters) and "Les Trois Sœurs ont voulu mourir" (The Three Sisters Wanted to Die)...' ('Chekhov's "Modern Classicism"', *The Slavonic and East European Review* 65, 1 [January 1987], pp. 20, 22-3).

65 Martin Esslin, 'Chekhov and the Modern Drama', in *A Chekhov Companion*, edited by Toby W. Clyman (Westport, Connecticut, and London, 1985), pp. 143-4.

66 Laurence Senelick, *Anton Chekhov* (London, 1985), pp. 107, 110, 111.

Stage Productions

Three Sisters is not merely a literary text, to be analysed by the scholar from the safety of his study. It is a piece for the living theatre, and comes fully alive only when interpreted by actors on-stage. An early critic remarked:

> Tchekov's plays are as interesting to read as the work of any first-rate novelist. But in reading them, it is impossible to guess how effective they are on the stage, the delicate succession of subtle shades and half-tones, of hints, of which they are composed, the evocation of certain moods and feelings which it is impossible to define – all this one would think would disappear in the glare of the footlights, but the result is exactly the reverse. Tchekov's plays are a thousand times more interesting to see on the stage than they are to read...[1]

Productions in Russia

The première of *Three Sisters* took place at the Moscow Arts Theatre on 31 January 1901. This famous production, directed by K.S. Stanislavsky, Vl. I. Nemirovich-Danchenko and V.V. Luzhsky, with sets by V.A. Simov, offered a cast which included V.V. Luzhsky (Andrei), M.P. Lilina (Natasha), M.G. Savitskaya (Olga), O.L. Knipper (Masha), M.F. Andreeva (Irina), A.L. Vishnevsky (Kulygin), K.S. Stanislavsky (Vershinin), V.E. Meyerhold (Tuzenbakh), M.A. Gromov (Solyony), A.R. Artem (Chebutykin), I.A. Tikhomirov (Fedotik), I.M. Moskvin (Rodé), V.F. Gribunin (Ferapont), and M.A. Samarova (Anfisa).

Stanislavsky later maintained that the first-night audience reacted coolly to the play. Only Act I was 'a great success', and it took 'a long time' for *Three Sisters* to gain acceptance with the public.[2] Initial press reaction was

---

1 Maurice Baring, *Landmarks in Russian Literature* (London and New York, 1960), p. 184; book first published in 1910. The essay there on Chekhov's plays was reprinted from *New Quarterly* (1908).

2 K.S. Stanislavsky, *Moia zhizn' v iskusstve* (Moscow, 1926), p. 312. Elsewhere,

mixed – while some critics thought the play a 'major event', others found it too pessimistic and hopeless, a repetition of the gloom of *Uncle Vanya*. Chekhov's latest play puzzled some reviewers by the indistinctness of its plot and of the characters' motivation. Nevertheless, Vl.I. Nemirovich-Danchenko unequivocally asserts:

> In its ensemble work, its unity of execution, and its maturity of form, *Three Sisters* was always regarded in the theatre as our best production of a Chekhov play...[3]

Having missed the opening performances, Chekhov wrote to A.L. Vishnevsky on 23 March 1901: 'I'd really love to see *Three Sisters...*' His wish was granted later in the year, when he came to Moscow. On the morning of 21 September 1901 Chekhov attended a rehearsal of *Three Sisters* at the Moscow Arts Theatre, and then in the evening saw a public performance of the play for the first time. At the end of the second and fourth acts he appeared on stage to acknowledge the audience's tumultuous applause. Three days later he wrote to his Yalta friend, Dr L.V. Sredin:

> *Three Sisters* is going splendidly, brilliantly, much better than the actual text. I helped a little on the production side, handing out a bit of authorial criticism, and people say the play's going better now than last season...[4]

A critic remarks that '*Three Sisters* was perhaps the only performance of one of his plays which Chekhov accepted unconditionally'.[5]

Stanislavsky states that 'the public gradually appreciated all the beauty of this remarkable work only three years after the first performance' (K.S. Stanislavsky, *A.P. Chekhov v Moskovskom Khudozhestvennom teatre* [Moscow, 1947], p. 64). However, an early historian of the Moscow Arts Theatre disputes this latter claim, and declares that *Three Sisters* won the public's affection 'much sooner' – see Nikolai Efros, *'Tri sestry': P'esa A.P. Chekhova v postanovke Moskovskogo Khudozhestvennogo teatra* (Petersburg, 1919), p. 47.

3 In the album *Moskovskii Khudozhestvennyi teatr: P'esy A.P. Chekhova. Chaika. Diadia Vania. Tri sestry. Vishnevyi sad. Ivanov* (St Petersburg, 1914), pages unnumbered [p. 55]. In his book *Iz proshlogo* (Moscow, 1936, pp. 218-19) Nemirovich-Danchenko pays tribute to 'Stanislavsky's *mise en scène*'.

4 Chekhov is said to have given advice to V.V. Luzhsky (Andrei) and V.I. Kachalov (about to appear as Vershinin), and to have rehearsed the off-stage sound effects (alarm bells) for the fire in Act III.

5 M.N. Stroeva, in *K.S. Stanislavskii: Materialy, pis'ma, issledovaniia*

Over the past ninety years, this 1901 production has been described and analysed in minute detail, by participants and historians of the theatre. Photographs of the Moscow Arts Theatre première (and of many subsequent revivals) may be seen in numerous albums and monographs.

After the 1917 Bolshevik Revolution Chekhov's plays fell into ideological disfavour in Russia. They became regarded as archaic and irrelevant, and for many years were seldom performed.

Eventually, on 27 October 1938 the Moscow Arts Theatre solemnly celebrated its fortieth anniversary, with Stalin and Molotov perched in the theatre's official Government box.[6] In 1940 Nemirovich-Danchenko staged a major revival of *Three Sisters* at the Moscow Arts Theatre. Before rehearsals began, he identified as the 'core' of the play the characters' 'longing (*toska*) for a better life'.[7] According to one commentator, this production 'developed into a protest against the entire social system of Tsarist Russia'.[8] It was a 'Soviet', 'socialist' reading of Chekhov, stressing the 'active' basis of the play which was performed in a '*major* key'.[9]

Over the next few decades this production ('the best Chekhov performance on the Soviet stage')[10] proved remarkably durable.[11] Renewed by I.M. Raevsky, it impressed London audiences and critics in May 1958. This Moscow Arts Theatre version revealed the value of meticulous ensemble-playing, evocative sets (especially the avenue of trees in Act IV), and scrupulous attention to every detail of production.

Yet despite the abiding historical importance of the 1901 première directed by Stanislavsky and Nemirovich-Danchenko (and of the 1940 revival), there is no uniquely 'correct' way to stage Chekhov's play. Stanislavsky

---

(Moscow, 1955), p. 669.

6 Rather like Natasha and Protopopov, lording it over the Prozorov house in Act IV of *Three Sisters* [G. McV.]. See *Moskovskii Khudozhestvennyi teatr v illiustratsiiakh i dokumentakh: 1939-1943*, edited by V.E. Meskheteli (Moscow, 1945), pp. 293-7.

7 Vl. I. Nemirovich-Danchenko, '"Tri sestry"', in *Ezhegodnik Moskovskogo Khudozhestvennogo teatra: 1943*, edited by V.E. Meskheteli *et al.* (Moscow, 1945), p. 154.

8 N. Gorchakov, Introduction to *Anton Pavlovich Chekhov v teatre*, edited by E. Zenkevich (Moscow, 1955), p. 14.

9 M. Stroeva, *Chekhov i Khudozhestvennyi teatr: Rabota K.S. Stanislavskogo i Vl.I. Nemirovicha-Danchenko nad p'esami A.P. Chekhova* (Moscow, 1955), pp. 254-5.

10 Ibid., p. 260.

11 By 1 January 1974 it had been offered 872 times. The original 1901 production was performed 299 times.

himself commented on Chekhov's particular perception of the Prozorov house:

> He could not assist us in our work, in our search for the interior of the Prozorov house. One felt that he knew this house in detail, he had seen it, and yet he had completely failed to notice the nature of the rooms, furniture and objects filling the house, he just felt the atmosphere of each individual room, but not its walls. That's how a literary man perceives his environment...[12]

Accordingly, designers over the years have devised sets for *Three Sisters* ranging in style from the most meticulous and photographic 'realism' or 'naturalism' to the suggestive allusiveness of 'symbolism' and 'abstractionism'. Georgii Tovstonogov, having staged the play at the Leningrad Gorky (Bolshoi Dramatic) Theatre in 1965, later reflected:

> The one thing of which I became firmly convinced after our production of *Three Sisters* is that today's Chekhov will not tolerate one stage second wasted on the reproduction of everyday detail. Verisimilitude alone is not worth much today. If Chekhov is not played with the idea of finding out what lies behind the external reproduction of life, and of revealing what lies behind the words and daily trivia and verisimilitude, then all the theatre's efforts will be fruitless...[13]

Tovstonogov's deliberately 'cinematic' production made effective use of the revolving stage and small moving platforms.

Much more idiosyncratic was the version shown at Moscow's Taganka Theatre in 1981 (director Yury Lyubimov, assistant director Yury Pogrebnichko). Throughout, there was a deliberate emphasis on the 'theatrical' and on the chorus; a desire to show the characters ironically as depersonalised, almost dehumanised puppets. Musical accompaniment and stylised gestures and groupings replaced the usual subtlety of individual characterisation. In a sense, 'form' dominated over 'content'. Despite

---

12 K.S. Stanislavsky, *A.P. Chekhov v Moskovskom Khudozhestvennom teatre* (Moscow, 1947), p. 61.

13 Georgii Tovstonogov, 'Chekhov's "Three Sisters" at the Gorky Theatre', *The Drama Review* XIII, 2 (1968), p. 155.

moments of striking innovation, of theatrical flair and perceptiveness, this production seemed rather too mannered and eccentric, too cold and detached, to be 'ideal'.

Productions in Britain

Chekhov's penultimate play has established a remarkable reputation in British theatrical circles. It enjoys the love and esteem of actors, directors, audiences, and critics alike. A production in 1987 at the Albery Theatre in London advertised *Three Sisters* as 'the play of the century',[14] and Kenneth Tynan has written that 'the last act is, I suppose, the high-water mark of twentieth-century drama'.[15] In 1967 Laurence Olivier waxed lyrical in his 'Producer's Note' for *Three Sisters* at the National Theatre:

> In Chekhov we are all stars: but not selfish, glistening on our own. We are flocks of bright angels, *all* glorifying our sun – Chekhov.[16]

It took many years, however, before the 'sun' of Chekhov pierced the grey skies over Britain. Only gradually did insular initial bewilderment at the 'alien' Russian's 'melancholic' art give way to widespread enthusiasm and admiration. This painful process has been chronicled in a number of books, which record the changing fortunes of *Three Sisters* on the British stage, ever since the first production in English at the Royal Court Theatre in London on 7 and 8 March 1920.[17]

Theodore Komisarjevsky's 1926 production at the Barnes Theatre was

---

14 Albery Theatre publicity leaflet, quoting Michael Ratcliffe in *The Observer* (29 March 1987), p. 23.

15 Kenneth Tynan, *Tynan on Theatre* (Harmondsworth, 1964), p. 275.

16 Laurence Olivier, in the programme for *Three Sisters* at the National Theatre, London, 1967. Elsewhere, Olivier refers to 'my beloved *Three Sisters*', 'that divinest of plays' (*Confessions of an Actor* [London, 1982], pp. 227, 226). The generally sensitive 1970 film of *Three Sisters* (with Olivier himself as Chebutykin and Joan Plowright as Masha) contained some ill-judged interpolations – above all, an explicit 'dream sequence' at the end of Act III, depicting Irina's vision of a glorious life in Moscow.

17 There were major London productions of *Three Sisters* in 1926, 1929, 1935, 1938 and 1951. Since 1967 revivals have become increasingly frequent. See *Chekhov: The Critical Heritage*, edited by Victor Emeljanow (London, Boston and Henley, 1981); *File on Chekhov*, compiled by Nick Worrall (London and New York, 1986); Patrick Miles, *Chekhov on the British Stage 1909-1987* (England, 1987); *Chekhov on the British Stage*, edited by Patrick Miles (Cambridge, 1993).

widely acclaimed. Admittedly, to facilitate Chekhov's acceptance by the British theatrical public, Komisarjevsky occasionally tampered with the original text, making it more conventional and easily comprehensible. Thus, among numerous cuts and embellishments, he omitted all reference to Tuzenbakh's ugliness, concealed the characters' ages, placed Protopopov physically on-stage during Act IV, and curiously transferred the entire action to the early 1870s.

The most illustrious British production of *Three Sisters* opened at the Queen's Theatre in London on 28 January 1938. Directed by Michel Saint-Denis and designed by Motley, it offered a cast which included George Devine (Andrei), Angela Baddeley (Natasha), Gwen Ffrangcon-Davies (Olga), Carol Goodner (Masha), Peggy Ashcroft (Irina), Leon Quartermaine (Kulygin), John Gielgud (Vershinin), Michael Redgrave (Tuzenbakh), Glen Byam Shaw (Solyony), Frederick Lloyd (Chebutykin), Alec Guinness (Fedotik), Harry Andrews (Rodé), George Howe (Ferapont), and Marie Wright (Anfisa). The brilliance of this production and cast remains unsurpassed.[18]

Beginning with the Moscow Arts Theatre's visit to London in 1958, the present writer has seen more than twenty productions of *Three Sisters* in England and Russia. The experience of these performances (and of life as a whole) has helped to shape the interpretation offered in Part One of this book. Virtually every production enriches the onlooker's critical perception – through a previously unconsidered detail of dialogue or characterisation, an unsuspected gesture or intonation, a nuance of pace or mood. The theatre-goer is free to accept or reject the creative imagination (and, at times, the arbitrary inventiveness) of each individual actor, director or designer.

Perhaps the most memorable English-language *Three Sisters* in recent years was Trevor Nunn's version for the Royal Shakespeare Company, designed by John Napier.[19] This production was remarkably fluid, conveying space and depth, and masterfully slowing the pace when necessary (the long pauses and frozen *tableaux*, the hum of the spinning-top, the posing for photographs, the snatches of song). Seated at floor-level, the audience was afforded an unusual sense of intimacy, as if actually inside the room with the characters. A huge brooding backcloth of Old Russian saints' heads looked down upon the excellent ensemble.

In the British theatre today there is a danger of over-emphasising the

---

18 See *Chekhov on the British Stage* (Cambridge, 1993), pp. 85-9.

19 The first performances of this production were: Small Scale Tour, 28 July 1978; The Other Place, Stratford-upon-Avon, 29 September 1979; The Warehouse, London, 2 April 1980. A recording of Trevor Nunn's version was shown on ITV on 29 December 1981.

'ironic' and 'hard' aspects of Chekhov's supposed attitude towards his characters, their thoughts and emotions. This is presumably a reaction against other extremes, such as the excessively sentimentalised, 'autumnal', tearful, or tragic Chekhov of earlier productions – but it remains a disservice to the author merely to replace one extreme by another. Some versions of *Three Sisters* have been predominantly cool, detached, anti-romantic and unsentimental, whether filtered through the intelligence of Jonathan Miller (Cambridge Theatre, 1976) or the sensitivity of Mike Alfreds (Bloomsbury, 1986), or, less palatably, via the harsh gaze of Elijah Moshinsky (Greenwich and Albery, 1987).

Most 'unChekhovian' of all was the *Three Sisters* presented by the Georgian Robert Sturua (Queen's Theatre, 1990). Too loud, too fast, too physical and too crude, this controversial production flaunted a pantomimic brashness. Under Sturua's manic direction, the characters seemed unable to sit still, speak quietly, or stay physically aloof. While Sturua's version certainly looked and sounded 'different', it remains an act of cultural barbarism.

It seems fitting to end this brief survey of British renditions by returning to the 'most legendary of all English Chekhov productions'.[20] Michel Saint-Denis' *Three Sisters* at the Queen's Theatre in 1938 seems to have blended production and acting, costumes and scenery, sound effects and lighting in rare perfection. Happy the critic who witnessed such a performance, and found the words to capture it. Lionel Hale reports:

> It was on Friday night that I saw Tchehov's 'Three Sisters' at the Queen's Theatre; and its people follow me still.
>
> If I shut my eyes I can see the tall, nearly shabby rooms of that provincial town in Russia, its oil-lamps, its gaunt wardrobes, the sunshine fitfully falling in at the window; I can hear its sounds, the sleigh-bells outside, the scrape of Prozorov's violin in the next room, the click of spurred heels, the rustle of Irina's dress as she turns in her chair, the rise and fall of the eddying, endless talk.
>
> Not to be niggardly, we shall never see this production of 'Three Sisters' surpassed; and we owe homage to the genius of M. Michel St.-Denis that has given it to us.
>
> He has caught – how deeply, how delicately! – the

20 Irving Wardle, at the Anglo-Soviet Colloquium, 'Chekhov on the British Stage', Cambridge, 5 August 1987.

atmosphere of that provincial town. The lives of the groups of exiles are running out like a trickle of water. They reach for happiness, but cannot close their hand on it. Ambitions of doctor, schoolmaster, Government official, soldier, are lost in a mist of dreams, of laughter, talk, drink, idleness, vanishing hourly, always more and more faintly seen.

'To Moscow!' cries Irina, and we know, and she soon knows, that they will never get to Moscow. We know and she knows that, should they get to Moscow, they will not escape themselves even there. Their dream is a toy; but, when it is broken, it has all the pathos and littleness of a broken toy.

Oh, M. St.-Denis knows these people; and he can play with exquisite modulations on their fits of temper, their childish kindnesses to one another, their self-tormenting talk, so that sudden laughter shakes out of our eyes the tears that have been gathering...

He is fortunate in having to his hand Mr. John Gielgud's company, a constellation of actors and actresses without thought of personal vanity...

We shall have great memories of them – of Masha (Miss Carol Goodner) sitting on the sofa, half-listening to Irina's slow outburst against the loveless life in which she is withering, sitting there with a little, dark, soft, wanton and secret smile as her love for Vershinin warms her until it breaks into flame and she must speak of it.

We shall remember the exquisitely faithful play of look and word between Olga (Miss Gwen Ffrangcon-Davies) and Irina (Miss Peggy Ashcroft) and the sketch of that soft and ruthless snob Natasha (Miss Angela Baddeley) to which, whenever we look again, we see that another stroke has been added.

We shall remember that most moving scene in which, in bed behind their screens, Irina and Olga lie in hard silence while their brother (Mr. George Devine) tries gallantly to excuse himself and his life, until his words, rebounding from those inexorable screens, fly into his face in all their falseness and he breaks down and hurries from the unpitying room.

We shall remember the coltish and bouncing Tusenbach, a brilliantly caressing piece of portraiture by Mr. Michael Redgrave, and the doctor of Mr. Frederick Lloyd, and the perfumed violence of Mr. Glen Byam Shaw's Solyony...

We shall remember how Mr. Leon Quartermaine as the schoolmaster, at that tiny and tremendous moment when he tries to amuse his wife, whose life is in ruins, with a false beard confiscated from a boy, caught us between laughter and tears...

To spend an evening with them is to be moved with heartache and laughter, pity, irritation, tenderness; and, when the curtain falls and we are out in Shaftesbury Avenue, it is the buses and the sky-signs and the bowler hats that are things of a dream.

It is the house that is real, and the drunken old doctor washing his hands, and Prozorov wheeling the perambulator in the autumnal garden which his wife will soon destroy, and Tusenbach going in a straw hat to his duel and his death, and Masha sitting heavy-lidded on the sofa, wearing her small, dark smile.[21]

---

21 Lionel Hale, *News Chronicle* (Tuesday 1 February 1938), p. 9.

Front cover of the first separate edition of *Three Sisters* (published by A.F. Marks, St Petersburg, 1901).

The cover shows portraits of the first Moscow Arts Theatre performers:

Top row (left to right): M.G. Savitskaya (Olga), O.L. Knipper (Masha), M.F. Andreeva (Irina).
Below: V.V. Luzhsky (Andrei).

Bibliography

Editions of *Three Sisters* (in Russian)

Chekhov, Anton, *Tri sestry*, in the journal *Russkaia mysl'* 2 (Moscow, 1901) pp. 124-78.

Chekhov, Anton, *Tri sestry: Drama v 4-kh deistviiakh* (Izdanie A.F. Marksa: St Petersburg, 1901). Further publications in 1902.

Chekhov, A.P., *Polnoe sobranie sochinenii i pisem v tridtsati tomakh* (Nauka: Moscow, 1974-83), works in eighteen volumes, letters in twelve volumes. Vol. 13 of the works (1978) contains the text of *Tri sestry*, with variants and detailed notes.

Chekhov, A.P., *Tri sestry/Three Sisters*, edited by J.M.C. Davidson (Bristol Classical Press, 1991/Blackwell Russian Texts: Oxford, 1984; formerly Bradda Books: Letchworth, 1962).

Translations of *Three Sisters* (in English)

Tchehov, Anton, *Three Sisters and Other Plays*, translated by Constance Garnett (Chatto & Windus: London, 1923).

Chekhov, Anton, *Plays*, translated and introduced by Elisaveta Fen (Penguin Books: Harmondsworth, 1959; the translation of *Three Sisters* first appeared in 1951).

[Chekhov, Anton], *Six Plays of Chekhov*, translated and introduced by Robert W. Corrigan (Holt, Rinehart and Winston: New York, 1962).

[Chekhov, Anton], *The Oxford Chekhov*, Volume III, translated and edited by Ronald Hingley (Oxford University Press: London, New York, Toronto, 1964).

[Chekhov, Anton], *Chekhov: The Major Plays*, translated by Ann Dunnigan, with a foreword by Robert Brustein (A Signet Classic, The New American Library: New York, 1964).

[Chekhov, Anton], *Anton Chekhov's Plays*, translated and edited by Eugene K. Bristow (A Norton Critical Edition, W.W. Norton & Company: New York and London, 1977).

Chekhov, Anton, *Three Sisters*, translated and introduced by Michael Frayn (Methuen: London and New York, 1983).

Chekhov, Anton, *Three Sisters*, a version by Frank McGuinness from a literal translation by Rose Cullen (Faber & Faber: London and Boston, 1990).

Chekhov, Anton, *Three Sisters*, translated by Paul Schmidt (TCG Translations: New York, 1992).

[Chekhov, Anton], *Chekhov for the Stage*, translated by Milton Ehre (Northwestern University Press: Evanston, Illinois, 1992).

Chekhov, Anton, *Three Sisters*, translated and introduced by Stephen Mulrine (Drama Classics, Nick Hern Books: London, 1994).

There are many other English translations of the play.

Secondary sources (in English)

Books, articles, and reviews

Agate, James, [review of *Three Sisters*], *The Sunday Times* (30 January 1938).

Baring, Maurice, *Landmarks in Russian Literature* (Methuen: London, 1910; republished University Paperbacks, Methuen: London and Barnes & Noble: New York, 1960).

Barricelli, Jean-Pierre (ed.), *Chekhov's Great Plays: A Critical Anthology* (New York University Press: New York and London, 1981) – see entries under Bristow, Karlinsky, Kramer, Moravčevich, Senelick and Valency.

Benedetti, Jean, *Stanislavski* (Methuen: London, 1988).

Benedetti, Jean (translator and ed.), *The Moscow Art Theatre Letters* (Methuen Drama: London, 1991).

Bermel, Albert, *Contradictory Characters: An Interpretation of the Modern Theatre* (E.P. Dutton & Co.: New York, 1973).

Brahms, Caryl, *Reflections in a Lake: A Study of Chekhov's Four Greatest Plays* (Weidenfeld and Nicolson: London, 1976).

Bristow, Eugene K., 'Circles, Triads, and Parity in *The Three Sisters*', in *Chekhov's Great Plays: A Critical Anthology*, edited by Jean-Pierre Barricelli (New York University Press: New York and London, 1981) pp. 76-95.

Briusov, Valerii, 'Russian Literature', *The Athenaeum* 3847 (London, 20 July 1901) pp. 85-7.

Bruford, W.H., *Chekhov and his Russia: A Sociological Study* (Kegan Paul, Trench, Trubner & Co.: London, 1947).

Brustein, Robert, *The Theatre of Revolt* (Methuen: London, 1965).

Chudakov, A.P., *Chekhov's Poetics*, translated by Edwina Jannie Cruise and Donald Dragt (Ardis: Ann Arbor, 1983).

Clardy, Jesse V., and Clardy, Betty S., *The Superfluous Man in Russian Letters* (University Press of America: Washington, 1980).

Clyman, Toby W. (ed.), *A Chekhov Companion* (Greenwood Press: Westport, Connecticut and London: 1985) – see entries under Esslin, Lantz, Pitcher, Senelick and Styan.

De Maegd-Soëp, Carolina, *Chekhov and Women: Women in the Life and Work of Chekhov* (Slavica Publishers: Ohio, 1987).

Egri, Péter, *Chekhov and O'Neill: The Uses of the Short Story in Chekhov's and O'Neill's Plays* (Akadémiai Kiadó: Budapest, 1986).

Elton, Oliver, *Chekhov* (The Clarendon Press: Oxford, 1929).

Emeljanow, Victor (ed.), *Chekhov: The Critical Heritage* (Routledge and Kegan Paul: London, Boston and Henley, 1981).

Emeljanow, Victor, 'Komisarjevsky Directs Chekhov in London', *Theatre Notebook* XXXVII, 2 (London, 1983) pp. 66-77.

Emeljanow, Victor, 'Komisarjevsky's *Three Sisters*: The Prompt Book', *Theatre Notebook* XLI, 2 (London, 1987) pp. 56-66.

Esslin, Martin, 'Chekhov and the Modern Drama', in *A Chekhov Companion*, edited by Toby W. Clyman (Greenwood Press: Westport, Connecticut and London, 1985) pp. 135-45.

Gerhardi, William, *Futility: A Novel on Russian Themes* (Richard Cobden-Sanderson: London, 1922; revised definitive collected edition [under the surname Gerhardie], Macdonald: London, 1971).

Gerhardi, William, *Anton Chehov: A Critical Study* (Richard Cobden-Sanderson: London, 1923; revised definitive collected edition [under the surname Gerhardie], Macdonald: London, 1974).

Gillès, Daniel, *Chekhov: Observer Without Illusion*, translated from the French by Charles Lam Markmann (Funk & Wagnalls: New York, 1968).

Gilman, Richard, *The Making of Modern Drama: A Study of Büchner, Ibsen, Strindberg, Chekhov, Pirandello, Brecht, Beckett, Handke* (Farrar, Straus and Giroux: New York, 1974).

Golomb, Harai, 'Communicating Relationships in Chekhov's *Three Sisters*', *Russian Language Journal* XXXIX, 132-4 (East Lansing, Michigan, 1985) pp. 53-77; reprinted in *Anton Chekhov Rediscovered: A Collection of New Studies With a Comprehensive Bibliography*, edited by Savely Senderovich and Munir Sendich (East Lansing, Michigan, 1987) pp. 9-33.

Golomb, Harai, 'A Badenweiler View of Chekhov's End(ings): Beyond the Final *Pointe* in His stories, Plays and Life (An Autobiographophobic Paper)', in *Anton P. Čechov: Werk und Wirkung* I, edited by Rolf-Dieter Kluge (Otto Harrassowitz: Wiesbaden, 1990) pp. 232-53.

Gottlieb, Vera, *Chekhov and the Vaudeville: A Study of Chekhov's One-Act Plays* (Cambridge University Press: Cambridge, 1982).

Hahn, Beverly, 'Chekhov: *The Three Sisters*', *The Critical Review* 15 (Melbourne, 1972) pp. 3-22.

Hahn, Beverly, *Chekhov: A Study of the Major Stories and Plays* (Cambridge University Press: Cambridge, 1977).

Hale, Lionel, [review of *Three Sisters*], *News Chronicle* (1 February 1938) p. 9.

Jackson, Robert Louis (ed.), *Chekhov: A Collection of Critical Essays* (Prentice-Hall, Inc.: Englewood Cliffs, N.J., 1967).

Jones, W. Gareth, 'Chekhov's Undercurrent of Time', *The Modern Language Review* 64, 1 (January 1969) pp. 111-21.

[Karlinsky, Simon], *Letters of Anton Chekhov*, translated by Michael Henry Heim in collaboration with Simon Karlinsky, selection, commentary and introduction by Simon Karlinsky (Harper & Row: New York, and The Bodley Head: London, 1973; republished as *Anton Chekhov's Life and Thought: Selected Letters and Commentary* [University of California Press: Berkeley, Los Angeles, London, 1975]).

Karlinsky, Simon, 'Huntsmen, Birds, Forests, and Three Sisters', in *Chekhov's Great Plays: A Critical Anthology*, edited by Jean-Pierre Barricelli (New York University Press: New York and London, 1981) pp. 144-60.

Karlinsky, Simon, 'Russian Anti-Chekhovians', *Russian Literature* XV (North-Holland, 1984) pp. 183-202.

Kerr, Walter, *Tragedy and Comedy* (Simon & Schuster: New York, 1967; The Bodley Head: London, 1968).

Komisarjevsky, Theodore, *Myself and the Theatre* (William Heinemann Limited: London, 1929).

Kramer, Karl D., '*Three Sisters*, or Taking a Chance on Love', in *Chekhov's Great Plays: A Critical Anthology*, edited by Jean-Pierre Barricelli (New York University Press: New York and London, 1981) pp. 61-75.

Kramer. Karl D., 'Passivity in Dying: Tuzenbakh and the Bishop', in *Anton P. Čechov: Werk und Wirkung* I, edited by Rolf-Dieter Kluge (Otto Harrassowitz: Wiesbaden, 1990) pp. 487-500.

Lantz, K.A., *Anton Chekhov: A Reference Guide to Literature* (G.K. Hall & Co.: Boston, Mass., 1985).

Lantz, Kenneth A., 'Chekhov's Cast of Characters', in *A Chekhov Companion*, edited by Toby W. Clyman (Greenwood Press: Westport, Connecticut and London, 1985) pp. 71-85.

Llewellyn Smith, Virginia, *Anton Chekhov and the Lady with the Dog* (Oxford University Press: London, New York, Toronto, 1973).

MacCarthy, Desmond, [review of *Three Sisters*], *The New Statesman and Nation* (5 February 1938) p. 206.

Magarshack, David, *Chekhov the Dramatist* (John Lehmann: London, 1952; republished, Eyre Methuen: London, 1980).

Magarshack, David, *The Real Chekhov: An Introduction to Chekhov's Last Plays* (George Allen & Unwin Ltd.: London, 1972).

Martin, Graham, *'Three Sisters', 'The Cherry Orchard' by Anton Chekhov* (The Open University Press: Milton Keynes, 1977).

McCarthy, Mary, *Sights and Spectacles 1937-1958* (Heinemann: London, 1959) especially pp. 55-60 (on *Three Sisters*, first published in *Partisan Review* X [1943] pp. 184-6).

McVay, Gordon, 'Chekhov's Last Two Stories: Dreaming of Happiness', in *The Short Story in Russia 1900-1917*, edited by Nicholas Luker (Astra Press: Nottingham, 1991) pp. 1-21.

McVay, Gordon, 'Chekhov's *Three Sisters*: Longing for the Ideal', *Rusistika* 3 (June 1991) pp. 2-7.

McVay, Gordon, '*The Three Sisters*', in *International Dictionary of Theatre I: Plays*, edited by Mark Hawkins-Dady (St James Press: Chicago and London, 1992) pp. 795-7.

McVay, Gordon, 'Peggy Ashcroft and Chekhov', in *Chekhov on the British Stage*, edited by Patrick Miles (Cambridge University Press: Cambridge, 1993) pp. 78-100.

McVay, Gordon (translator and ed.), *Chekhov: A Life in Letters* (The Folio Society: London, 1994).

Meister, Charles W., *Chekhov Bibliography: Works in English by and about Anton Chekhov; American, British and Canadian Performances* (McFarland & Company, Inc.: Jefferson, North Carolina and London, 1985).

Meister, Charles W., *Chekhov Criticism: 1880 Through 1986* (McFarland & Company, Inc.: Jefferson, North Carolina and London, 1988).

Melchinger, Siegfried, *Anton Chekhov*, translated by Edith Tarcov (Frederick Ungar Publishing Co.: New York, 1972).

Miles, Patrick, *Chekhov on the British Stage 1909-1987* (Sam & Sam: England, 1987).

Miles, Patrick (ed.), *Chekhov on the British Stage* (Cambridge University Press: Cambridge, 1993).

Mirsky, Prince D.S., *Modern Russian Literature* (Oxford University Press: London, 1925; reprinted, Haskell House: New York, 1974).

Mirsky, Prince D.S., *Contemporary Russian Literature 1881-1925* (George Routledge & Sons: London, and Alfred A. Knopf: New York, 1926; reprinted, Klaus Reprint: New York, 1972).

Mirsky, D.S., 'Chekhov and the English', *The Monthly Criterion* VI, 4 (October 1927) pp. 292-304.

Moravčevich, Nicholas, 'Women in Chekhov's Plays', in *Chekhov's Great Plays: A Critical Anthology*, edited by Jean-Pierre Barricelli (New York University Press: New York and London, 1981) pp. 201-17.

Moss, Howard, '*Three Sisters*', *The Hudson Review* XXX, 4 (Winter 1977-78) pp. 525-43.

Murry, John Middleton, 'Religion and Faith', *The Adelphi* 1, 3 (August 1923) pp. 177-84.

Nemirovitch-Dantchenko, Vladimir, *My Life in the Russian Theatre*, translated by John Cournos (Little, Brown: Boston, 1936; Geoffrey Bles: London, 1937).

Nilsson, Nils Åke, 'Intonation and Rhythm in Čechov's Plays', in *Anton Čechov: 1860-1960. Some Essays*, edited by T. Eekman (E.J. Brill: Leiden, 1960) pp. 168-80.

Olivier, Laurence, 'Producer's Note', in the programme for *Three Sisters* at the National Theatre, London, 1967.

Olivier, Laurence, *Confessions of an Actor* (Weidenfeld and Nicolson: London, 1982).

Parker, David, 'Three Men in Chekhov's *Three Sisters*', *The Critical Review* 21 (Melbourne, 1979) pp. 11-23.

Peace, Richard, *Chekhov: A Study of the Four Major Plays* (Yale University Press: New Haven and London, 1983).

Peace, Richard, 'Chekhov's "Modern Classicism"', *The Slavonic and East European Review* 65, 1 (January 1987) pp. 13-25.

Peacock, Ronald, *The Poet in the Theatre* (Routledge: London, 1946).

Pitcher, Harvey, *The Chekhov Play: A New Interpretation* (Chatto & Windus: London, 1973).

Pitcher, Harvey, *Chekhov's Leading Lady: A Portrait of the Actress Olga Knipper* (John Murray: London, 1979).

Pitcher, Harvey, 'Chekhov's Humour', in *A Chekhov Companion*, edited by Toby W. Clyman (Greenwood Press: Westport, Connecticut and London, 1985) pp. 87-103.

Proffer, Carl R., and Meyer, Ronald, *Nineteenth-Century Russian Literature in English: A Bibliography of Criticism and Translations* (Ardis: Ann Arbor, 1990) pp. 33-52.

Rayfield, Donald, *Chekhov: The Evolution of his Art* (Paul Elek: London, 1975).

Rayfield, Donald, 'Chekhov and Popular Culture', *Irish Slavonic Studies* 9 (Dublin, 1988) pp. 47-60.

Rokem, Freddie, *Theatrical Space in Ibsen, Chekhov and Strindberg: Public Forms of Privacy* (UMI Research Press: Ann Arbor, 1986).

Sendich, Munir, 'Anton Chekhov in English: A Comprehensive Bibliography of Works About and By Him (1889-1984)', *Russian Language Journal* XXXIX, 132-4 (East Lansing, Michigan, 1985) pp. 227-389; revised version, in *Anton Chekhov Rediscovered: A Collection of New Studies With a Comprehensive Bibliography*, edited by Savely Senderovich and Munir Sendich (Russian Language Journal: East Lansing, Michigan, 1987) pp. 189-349.

Senelick, Laurence, 'Chekhov's Drama, Maeterlinck, and the Russian Symbolists', in *Chekhov's Great Plays: A Critical Anthology*, edited by Jean-Pierre Barricelli (New York University Press: New York and London, 1981) pp. 161-80.

Senelick, Laurence, *Anton Chekhov* (Macmillan: London, 1985).

Senelick, Laurence, 'Chekhov on Stage', in *A Chekhov Companion*, edited by Toby W. Clyman (Greenwood Press: Westport, Connecticut and London, 1985) pp. 209-32.

Shestov, Leon [Lev], 'Anton Tchekhov (Creation from the Void)', in his *Chekhov and Other Essays*, new introduction by Sidney Monas (Ann Arbor Paperbacks, The University of Michigan Press: Ann Arbor, 1966) pp. 3-60 (translation first published, 1916).

Simmons, Ernest J., *Chekhov: A Biography* (Little, Brown and Company: Boston and Toronto, 1962; Jonathan Cape: London, 1963).

Speirs, Logan, *Tolstoy and Chekhov* (Cambridge University Press: Cambridge, 1971).

Stanislavsky, Constantin, *My Life in Art*, translated by J.J. Robbins (Little, Brown, and Company: Boston, and Geoffrey Bles: London, 1924).

Steiner, George, *The Death of Tragedy* (Faber & Faber: London, 1961).

Stenberg, Douglas G., '"It Seems To Matter": Linguistic Opposition in Chekhov's *The Three Sisters*', *Irish Slavonic Studies* 10 (Dublin, 1989 [1991]) pp. 41-6.

Stowell, H. Peter, *Literary Impressionism, James and Chekhov* (The University of Georgia Press: Athens, USA, 1980).

Styan, J.L., *The Elements of Drama* (Cambridge University Press: Cambridge, 1960).

Styan, J.L., *Chekhov in Performance: A Commentary on the Major Plays* (Cambridge University Press: Cambridge, 1971).

Styan, J.L., 'Chekhov's Dramatic Technique', in *A Chekhov Companion*, edited by Toby W. Clyman (Greenwood Press: Westport, Connecticut and London, 1985) pp. 107-22.

Timmer, Charles B., 'The Bizarre Element in Čechov's Art', in *Anton Čechov: 1860-1960. Some Essays*, edited by T. Eekman (E.J. Brill: Leiden, 1960) pp. 277-92.

Toumanova, Princess Nina Andronikova, *Anton Chekhov: The Voice of Twilight Russia* (Columbia University Press: New York, 1937; reprinted, 1960).

Tovstonogov, Georgii, 'Chekhov's "Three Sisters" at the Gorky Theatre', translated by Joyce C. Vining, *The Drama Review* XIII, 2 (New York, Winter 1968) pp. 146-55.

Tracy, Robert, 'Komisarjevsky's 1926 *Three Sisters*', in *Chekhov on the British Stage*, edited by Patrick Miles (Cambridge University Press: Cambridge, 1993) pp. 65-77.

Trilling, Lionel, 'The Three Sisters', in his *Prefaces to The Experience of Literature* (Harcourt Brace Jovanovich: New York and London, 1979 [first published 1967]) pp. 28-36.

Tulloch, John, *Chekhov: A Structuralist Study* (Macmillan: London, 1980).

Turner, C.J.G., 'Time in Chekhov's *Tri sestry*', *Canadian Slavonic Papers* XXVIII, 1 (March 1986) pp. 64-79.

Turner, C.J.G., *Time and Temporal Structure in Chekhov* (Birmingham Slavonic Monographs No. 22: Birmingham, 1994).

Tynan, Kenneth, *Tynan on Theatre* (Penguin Books: Harmondsworth, 1964).

Valency, Maurice, *The Breaking String: The Plays of Anton Chekhov* (Oxford University Press: New York, 1966).

Valency, Maurice, 'Vershinin', in *Chekhov's Great Plays: A Critical Anthology*, edited by Jean-Pierre Barricelli (New York University Press: New York and London, 1981) pp. 218-32.

Walter, Harriet, 'Chasing Chekhov', *Drama* 169 (London, 1988) pp. 27-30.

Walton, Michael, '"If Only We Knew"', *New Theatre Magazine* 8, 1 (Bristol, Autumn 1968) pp. 29-35.

Wellek, René, 'Introduction: Chekhov in English and American Criticism', in *Chekhov: New Perspectives*, edited by René and Nonna D. Wellek (Prentice Hall, Inc.: Englewood Cliffs, N.J., 1984) pp. 1-30.

Whitaker, Thomas R., *Fields of Play in Modern Drama* (Princeton University Press: Princeton, 1977).

Wiles, Timothy J., *The Theater Event: Modern Theories of Performance* (University of Chicago Press: Chicago and London, 1980).

Woolf, Virginia, *The Common Reader* [First Series] (The Hogarth Press: London, 1925; various reprints).

Worrall, Nick (compiler), *File on Chekhov* (Methuen: London and New York, 1986).

Worrall, Nick, 'Stanislavsky's Production of Chekhov's *Three Sisters*', in *Russian Theatre in the Age of Modernism*, edited by Robert Russell and Andrew Barratt (Macmillan: London, 1990) pp. 1-32.

Yermilov [Ermilov], Vladimir, *Anton Pavlovich Chekhov 1860-1904*, translated from the Russian by Ivy Litvinov (Foreign Languages Publishing House: Moscow, no date [1956?]).

Secondary sources (in Russian)

[The transliteration system employed in the Bibliography differs slightly from that used in the main body of the book.]

Books and articles

Aikhenval'd, Iu., *Siluety russkikh pisatelei: Vypusk I*, revised third edition

(Nauchnoe slovo: Moscow, 1911).

Andreev, Leonid, 'Tri sestry', in *Polnoe sobranie sochinenii Leonida Andreeva* VI (A.F. Marks: St Petersburg, 1913) pp. 321-5.

Annenskii, I.F., *Kniga otrazhenii* (Trud: St Petersburg, 1906; reprinted, as part of *Knigi otrazhenii I, II*, Wilhelm Fink: Munich, 1969).

Annenskii, Innokentii, *Knigi otrazhenii* (Nauka: Moscow, 1979).

Balukhatyi, S., *Problemy dramaturgicheskogo analiza: Chekhov* (Academia: Leningrad, 1927; reprinted, Wilhelm Fink: Munich, 1969).

Balukhatyi, S., *Chekhov dramaturg* (Khudozhestvennaia literatura: Leningrad, 1936).

Belyi, Andrei, *Arabeski: Kniga statei* (Musaget: Moscow, 1911; reprint, Wilhelm Fink: Munich, 1969).

Berdnikov, G.P., *Anton Pavlovich Chekhov: 1860-1904* [in the series 'Russkie dramaturgi: Nauchno-populiarnye ocherki'] (Iskusstvo: Moscow-Leningrad, 1950).

Berdnikov, G., *A.P. Chekhov: Ideinye i tvorcheskie iskaniia* (Gosudarstvennoe izdatel'stvo khudozhestvennoi literatury: Moscow-Leningrad, 1961; revised second edition, Khudozhestvennaia literatura: Leningrad, 1970; revised third edition, Khudozhestvennaia literatura: Moscow, 1984).

Berdnikov, G., *Chekhov-dramaturg: Traditsii i novatorstvo v dramaturgii A.P. Chekhova*, revised third edition (Iskusstvo: Moscow, 1981) [first edition, Iskusstvo: Moscow-Leningrad, 1957].

Berdnikov, G., *Izbrannye raboty v dvukh tomakh* (Khudozhestvennaia literatura: Moscow, 1986).

Bialyi, G.A., 'Chekhov', in the volume *Istoriia russkoi literatury* IX, 2 (Izdatel'stvo Akademii Nauk SSSR: Moscow-Leningrad, 1956).

Bialyi, G., *Chekhov i russkii realizm: Ocherki* (Sovetskii pisatel': Leningrad, 1981).

Blok, Aleksandr, *Sobranie sochinenii v vos'mi tomakh* V-VIII (Gosudarstvennoe izdatel'stvo khudozhestvennoi literatury: Moscow-Leningrad, 1962-3).

Briusov, Valerii, '"Vishnevyi sad" Chekhova', in *Literaturnoe nasledstvo*, LXXXV: *Valerii Briusov* (Nauka: Moscow, 1976) pp. 195-9 (introduced by E.A. Polotskaia, pp. 190-4).

Broide, E., *Chekhov: Myslitel'. Khudozhnik (100-letie tvorcheskogo puti). Katastrofa. Vozrozhdenie* (Polyglott-Druck: Frankfurt/Main, 1980).

Bulgakov, Professor S.N., *Chekhov kak myslitel'* (Izdanie literaturnogo kruzhka imeni A.P. Chekhova: Moscow, 1910).

Bunin, I.A., 'Iz zapisnoi knizhki', in *Chekhov v vospominaniiakh sovremennikov*, revised second edition, edited by A.K. Kotov (Gosudarstvennoe izdatel'stvo khudozhestvennoi literatury: Moscow, 1954) pp. 484-95.

Bunin, I.A., *O Chekhove: Nezakonchennaia rukopis'* (Izdatel'stvo imeni Chekhova: New York, 1955).

Chekhov, A.P., *Polnoe sobranie sochinenii i pisem v tridtsati tomakh*, works in eighteen volumes, letters in twelve volumes (Nauka: Moscow, 1974-83). Vol. 17 of the works (1980) contains Chekhov's notebooks.

Chekhov, M.P., *Vokrug Chekhova: Vstrechi i vpechatleniia*, revised fourth edition (Moskovskii rabochii: Moscow, 1964).

Chudakov, A.P., *Poetika Chekhova* (Nauka: Moscow, 1971).

Chudakov, A., *Mir Chekhova: Vozniknovenie i utverzhdenie* (Sovetskii pisatel': Moscow, 1986).

Chukovskii, K., *Ot Chekhova do nashikh dnei: Literaturnye portrety. Kharakteristiki*, third edition, revised and expanded (M.O. Vol'f: St Petersburg and Moscow, 1908).

Chukovskii, K., 'O Chekhove', in *Chekhovskii iubileinyi sbornik*, edited by M. Semenov and N. Tulupov (I.D. Sytin: Moscow, 1910) pp. 239-48.

Chukovskii, K., 'Chekhov i khristianstvo', *Mir* 5 (1910) pp. 356-9.

Chukovskii, Kornei, *O Chekhove* (Khudozhestvennaia literatura: Moscow, 1967).

Chushkin, N.N. (ed.), *Moskovskii Khudozhestvennyi teatr: Tom pervyi. 1898-1917* (Gosudarstvennoe izdatel'stvo izobrazitel'nogo iskusstva: Moscow, 1955).

Derman, A., *Tvorcheskii portret Chekhova* (Mir: Moscow, 1929).

Derman, A., *Anton Pavlovich Chekhov: Kritiko-biograficheskii ocherk* (Khudozhestvennaia literatura: Moscow, 1939).

Efros, N., and Nemirovich-Danchenko, Vl. (authors of the text), in the album *Moskovskii Khudozhestvennyi teatr: P'esy A.P. Chekhova. Chaika. Diadia Vania. Tri sestry. Vishnevyi sad. Ivanov* (Solntse Rossii: St Petersburg, 1914).

Efros, Nikolai, *K.S. Stanislavskii (Opyt kharakteristiki)* (Svetozar: Petersburg, 1918).

Efros, Nikolai, *V.I. Kachalov (Fragment)* (Svetozar: Petersburg, 1919).

Efros, Nikolai, *'Tri sestry' : P'esa A.P. Chekhova v postanovke Moskovskogo Khudozhestvennogo teatra*, foreword ['Ot redaktora'] by Vl. Nemirovich-Danchenko (Svetozar: Petersburg, 1919).

Efros, Nikolai, *Moskovskii Khudozhestvennyi teatr: 1898-1923* (Gosudarstvennoe izdatel'stvo: Moscow-Petersburg, 1924).

Ermilov, V., *A.P. Chekhov: Tvorcheskii portret* (Sovetskii pisatel': Moscow, 1944).

Ermilov, V., *Dramaturgiia Chekhova* (Sovetskii pisatel': Moscow, 1948).

Ermilov, V., *A.P. Chekhov* (Sovetskii pisatel': Moscow, 1954; revised edition, Sovetskii pisatel': Moscow, 1959).

Ermilov, V., *Izbrannye raboty v trekh tomakh* (Gosudarstvennoe izdatel'stvo khudozhestvennoi literatury: Moscow, 1955-6).

Feider, Val. (compiler), *A.P. Chekhov: Literaturnyi byt i tvorchestvo po memuarnym materialam* (Academia: Leningrad, 1928).

Gorchakov, N., Introduction to the album *Anton Pavlovich Chekhov v teatre*, edited by E. Zenkevich (Gosudarstvennoe izdatel′stvo izobrazitel′nogo iskusstva: Moscow, 1955).

Gor′kii, Maksim, 'A.P. Chekhov', in *M. Gor′kii i A. Chekhov: Perepiska. Stat′i. Vyskazyvaniia*, compiled by N.I. Gitovich (Gosudarstvennoe izdatel′stvo khudozhestvennoi literatury: Moscow, 1951) pp. 126-44.

Grigor′ev, M., *Stsenicheskaia kompozitsiia chekhovskikh p′es* (Izdanie KUBS'a V.L.Kh.I.: Moscow, 1924).

Gurliand, I.Ia. [Ars. G.], 'Iz vospominanii ob A.P. Chekhove', *Teatr i iskusstvo* 28 (11 July 1904) pp. 520-2.

Kalmanovskii, E., 'Sestry Prozorovy vchera, segodnia i zavtra', *Zvezda* 1 (1966) pp. 204-12.

Kamianov, V., *Vremia protiv bezvremen′ia: Chekhov i sovremennost′* (Sovetskii pisatel′: Moscow, 1989).

Kataev, V.B., *Literaturnye sviazi Chekhova* (Izdatel′stvo Moskovskogo universiteta: Moscow, 1989).

Kniazevskaia, T.B., 'Providcheskoe u Chekhova (Chetyre postanovki "Trekh sester")', in *Chekhoviana: Chekhov v kul′ture XX veka*, edited by V.B. Kataev *et al.* (Nauka: Moscow, 1993) pp. 130-6.

Knipper-Chekhova, O.L., 'O A.P. Chekhove', in *Chekhov v vospominaniiakh sovremennikov*, revised second edition, edited by A.K. Kotov (Gosudarstvennoe izdatel′stvo khudozhestvennoi literatury: Moscow, 1954) pp. 591-612.

Kostelianets, B., 'Chekhovskie katastrofy', in *Chekhov i teatral′noe iskusstvo: Sbornik nauchnykh trudov*, edited by A.A. Ninov *et al.* (Leningradskii gosudarstvennyi institut teatra, muzyki i kinematografii im. N.K. Cherkasova: Leningrad, 1985) pp. 65-96.

Kurdiumov, M., *Serdtse smiatennoe: O tvorchestve A.P. Chekhova. 1904-1934* (YMCA Press: Paris, 1934).

Lakshin, V., *Tolstoi i Chekhov* (Sovetskii pisatel′: Moscow, 1963; revised second edition, Sovetskii pisatel′: Moscow, 1975).

Lunacharskii, Anatolii, 'O khudozhnike voobshche i nekotorykh khudozhnikakh v chastnosti', *Russkaia mysl′* 2 (Moscow, 1903) especially pp. 58-60.

Maiakovskii, Vladimir, 'Dva Chekhova' [1914], *Polnoe sobranie sochinenii v trinadtsati tomakh* I (Gosudarstvennoe izdatel′stvo khudozhestvennoi literatury: Moscow, 1955) pp. 294-301.

Mandel′shtam, Osip, 'O p′ese A. Chekhova "Diadia Vania" (Nabrosok)' [1936], *Sobranie sochinenii* IV (YMCA-Press: Paris, 1981) pp. 107-9.

Meierkhol′d, V.E., *Perepiska: 1896-1939*, compiled by V.P. Korshunova and M.M. Sitkovetskaia (Iskusstvo: Moscow, 1976).

Merezhkovskii, D.S., *Chekhov i Gor'kii* (M.V. Pirozhkov: St Petersburg, 1906; reprint, Prideaux Press: Letchworth, 1975).

Meskheteli, V.E. (ed.), *Moskovskii Khudozhestvennyi teatr v illiustratsiiakh i dokumentakh: 1939-1943* (Izdanie Muzeia MKhAT: Moscow, 1945).

Natova, Nadezhda, 'Mechty geroev Chekhova o drugoi zhizni', *Zapiski russkoi akademicheskoi gruppy v SShA / Transactions of the Association of Russian-American Scholars in the U.S.A.* XVIII (New York, 1985) pp. 25-53.

Nekhoroshev, Iu.I., *Dekorator Khudozhestvennogo teatra Viktor Andreevich Simov* (Sovetskii khudozhnik: Moscow, 1984).

Nemirovich-Danchenko, Vl.Iv. – see Efros, Nikolai.

Nemirovich-Danchenko, Vl. Iv., *Iz proshlogo* (Academia: Moscow, 1936).

Nemirovich-Danchenko, Vl. I., '"Tri sestry"', in *Ezhegodnik Moskovskogo Khudozhestvennogo teatra: 1943*, edited by V.E. Meskheteli *et al.* (Izdanie Muzeia MKhAT: Moscow, 1945) pp. 149-57.

Nemirovich-Danchenko, Vl.I., *Rozhdenie teatra: Vospominaniia, stat'i, zametki, pis'ma*, compiled by M.N. Liubomudrov (Pravda: Moscow, 1989).

Papernyi, Z., *Zapisnye knizhki Chekhova* (Sovetskii pisatel': Moscow, 1976).

Papernyi, Z., *'Vopreki vsem pravilam...' : P'esy i vodevili Chekhova* (Iskusstvo: Moscow, 1982).

Papernyi, Z.S., '"Pravda bezuslovnaia i chestnaia"', in *Chekhov i literatura narodov Sovetskogo Soiuza*, edited by K.V. Aivazian *et al.* (Izdatel'stvo Erevanskogo universiteta: Erevan, 1982) pp. 143-64.

Papernyi, Z., *Strelka iskusstva* (Sovremennik: Moscow, 1986).

Polotskaia, E., *A.P. Chekhov: Dvizhenie khudozhestvennoi mysli* (Sovetskii pisatel': Moscow, 1979).

Polotskaia, E.A., *Puti chekhovskikh geroev* (Prosveshchenie: Moscow, 1983).

Roskin, A., *'Tri sestry' na stsene Khudozhestvennogo teatra* (Vserossiiskoe Teatral'noe Obshchestvo: Leningrad-Moscow, 1946).

Roskin, A., *A.P. Chekhov: Stat'i i ocherki* (Gosudarstvennoe izdatel'stvo khudozhestvennoi literatury: Moscow, 1959).

Roskin, A., 'Opasnosti i soblazny', *Teatr* 1 (Moscow, January 1960) pp. 110-16.

Rudnitskii, K., 'O poetike chekhovskoi dramy', *Teatr* 1 (Moscow, January 1960) pp. 117-27.

Sakharova, E.M., '"Vash A. Chekhov, sverkhshtatnyi plemiannik" (K tvorcheskoi istorii p'esy "Tri sestry")', in *Chekhoviana: Chekhov v kul'ture XX veka*, edited by V.B. Kataev *et al.* (Nauka: Moscow, 1993) pp. 76-83.

Shakh-Azizova, T.K., *Chekhov i zapadno-evropeiskaia drama ego vremeni* (Nauka: Moscow, 1966).

Shakh-Azizova, T.K., 'Sovremennoe prochtenie chekhovskikh p'es (60 – 70-e gody)', in *V tvorcheskoi laboratorii Chekhova*, edited by L.D. Opul'skaia, Z.S. Papernyi, S.E. Shatalov (Nauka: Moscow, 1974) pp. 336-53.

Shestov, Lev, 'Tvorchestvo iz nichego (A.P. Chekhov)', in his *Nachala i kontsy: Sbornik statei* (M.M. Stasiulevich: St Petersburg, 1908; reprinted, Ardis: Ann Arbor, 1978) pp. 1-68.

Skaftymov, A., *Nravstvennye iskaniia russkikh pisatelei: Stat'i i issledovaniia o russkikh klassikakh* (Khudozhestvennaia literatura: Moscow, 1972).

Solov'eva, I.N., '"Tri sestry" i "Vishnevyi sad" v Khudozhestvennom teatre', in *Rezhisserskie ekzempliary K.S. Stanislavskogo*, III: *1901-1904: P'esy A.P. Chekhova 'Tri sestry', 'Vishnevyi sad'* (Iskusstvo: Moscow, 1983) pp. 5-85.

Stanislavskii, K.S., *Moia zhizn' v iskusstve* (Gosudarstvennaia akademiia khudozhestvennykh nauk: Moscow, 1926).

Stanislavskii, K.S., *A.P. Chekhov v Moskovskom Khudozhestvennom teatre* ('Biblioteka Ezhegodnika Moskovskogo Khudozhestvennogo teatra', Izdanie Muzeia MKhAT: Moscow, 1947; first published in *Ezhegodnik Moskovskogo Khudozhestvennogo teatra: 1943*, edited by V.E. Meskheteli *et al.* [Izdanie Muzeia MKhAT: Moscow, 1945] pp. 95-148).

Stanislavskii, K.S., *Sobranie sochinenii v vos'mi tomakh*, VII: *Pis'ma 1886-1917* (Iskusstvo: Moscow, 1960).

[Stanislavskii, K.S.], *Rezhisserskie ekzempliary K.S. Stanislavskogo*, III: *1901-1904: P'esy A.P. Chekhova 'Tri sestry', 'Vishnevyi sad'* (Iskusstvo: Moscow, 1983) pp. 87-289.

Stroeva, M., *Chekhov i Khudozhestvennyi teatr: Rabota K.S. Stanislavskogo i Vl.I. Nemirovicha-Danchenko nad p'esami A.P. Chekhova* (Iskusstvo: Moscow, 1955).

Stroeva, M.N., 'Rezhissura K.S. Stanislavskogo v chekhovskikh spektakliakh MKhT: "Chaika", "Diadia Vania", "Tri sestry", 1898-1901 gg.', in *K.S. Stanislavskii: Materialy, pis'ma, issledovaniia* [*Teatral'noe nasledstvo* 1] (Izdatel'stvo Akademii nauk SSSR: Moscow, 1955) pp. 613-70.

Surkov, E.D. (compiler), *Chekhov i teatr: Pis'ma, fel'etony, sovremenniki o Chekhove-dramaturge* (Iskusstvo: Moscow, 1961).

[Suvorin, A.S.], *Dnevnik A.S. Suvorina*, edited by M. Krichevskii (Izdatel'stvo L.D. Frenkel': Moscow-Petrograd, 1923).

Tamarli, G.I., *Poetika dramaturgii A.P. Chekhova* (Izdatel'stvo Rostovskogo universiteta: Rostov-na-Donu, 1993).

Tovstonogov, G., *Besedy s kollegami (Popytka osmysleniia rezhisserskogo opyta)* (STD RSFSR: Moscow, 1988).

Turkov, A., *A.P. Chekhov i ego vremia* (Khudozhestvennaia literatura: Moscow, 1980; revised second edition, Sovetskaia Rossiia: Moscow, 1987).

Vladimirskaia, A.R., 'Dve rannie redaktsii p'esy "Tri sestry"', in *Literaturnoe nasledstvo*, LXVIII: *Chekhov* (Izdatel'stvo Akademii nauk SSSR: Moscow, 1960) pp. 1-86.

Vladimirskaia, A., 'Zametki na poliakh', *Teatr* 1 (Moscow, January 1960) pp. 157-9.

Zaitsev, Boris, *Chekhov: Literaturnaia biografiia* (Izdatel'stvo imeni Chekhova: New York, 1954).

Zalygin, Sergei, 'Moi poet', in his *Literaturnye zaboty*, revised third edition (Sovetskaia Rossiia: Moscow, 1982) pp. 344-435.

Zingerman, B., *Teatr Chekhova i ego mirovoe znachenie* (Nauka: Moscow, 1988).

Index

Other books available in the series:

Chekhov's *Uncle Vania* and *The Wood Demon* by D. Rayfield
Dostoyevsky's *Notes from Underground* by R. Peace
Pushkin's *Queen of Spades* by N. Cornwell
Tolstoy's *Childhood* by G. Williams

forthcoming:

Blok's *The Twelve* by J. Doherty
Gogol's *The Government Inspector* by M. Beresford
Gorky's *Lower Depths* by A. Barratt
Lermontov's *A Hero of our Time* by R. Reid
Pushkin's *The Bronze Horseman* by A. Kahn
Turgenev's *Fathers and Sons* by J. Woodward
Zamyatin's *We* by R. Russell

CPSIA information can be obtained
at www.ICGtesting.com
Printed in the USA
LVOW13s0019260518
578530LV00017B/266/P